School Administrator's
Handbook of Teacher Supervision
and Evaluation Methods

School Administrator's Handbook of Teacher Supervision and Evaluation Methods

RONALD T. HYMAN, Ed.D.

Professor of Education
Graduate School of Education
Rutgers University

PRENTICE-HALL, INC.   Englewood Cliffs, N.J.

Prentice-Hall International, Inc., *London*
Prentice-Hall of Australia, Pty. Ltd., *Sydney*
Prentice-Hall of Canada, Ltd., *Toronto*
Prentice-Hall of India Private Ltd., *New Delhi*
Prentice-Hall of Japan, Inc., *Tokyo*

© 1975 by
Prentice-Hall, Inc.
Englewood Cliffs, N.J.

Seventh Printing . . . . . October, 1979

Library of Congress Cataloging in Publication Data

Hyman, Ronald T.
  School administrator's handbook of teacher
supervision and evaluation methods.

  1. Teachers, Rating of. I. Title.
LB2838.H95   371.1'44   74-34301
ISBN 0-13-792382-1

Printed in the United States of America

Contents

Chapter 4

How to Observe and Improve Classroom Climate

Chapter 5

How to Observe and Improve Pedagogical Interaction Patterns

Chapter 5—How to Observe and Improve Pedagogical Interaction Patterns (cont.)

Chapter 6

How to Observe and Improve Cognitive Processes

The Verification Method

Chapter 7

How to Observe and Improve Classroom Use
of Space and Student Groupings

Chapter 7—How to Observe and Improve Classroom Use of Space and Student Groupings (cont.)

Chapter 8

**Teaching Strategies: What They Are
and How to Help Teachers with Them**

Chapter 9

How to Give Helpful Feedback

Chapter 10

How to Communicate Effectively

Chapter 11

How to Use a Simulation Game with Your Faculty

Chapter 11—How to Use a Simulation Game with Your Faculty (cont.)

Chapter 12

How to Utilize Brainstorming With Your Faculty

Chapter 13

How to Help Teachers Write Performance Objectives

School Administrator's
Handbook of Teacher Supervision
and Evaluation Methods

1

Introduction

This book is for supervisors—superintendents, principals, vice-principals, department chairpersons, elementary school coordinators, secondary school coordinators, and subject matter specialists—who have the task of working with teachers in our schools. This is a straightforward, practical book written for the supervisor who wants to know what and how to supervise. The book is designed around strategies, suggestions, meaningful examples, and usable materials. It is based on research and experience; it is not a theoretical book, although it is surely based on a theory of supervision which requires the supervisor to be knowledgeable and competent in his relations with teachers.

This book is based on a concept of supervision which sees the supervisor as a person of vision. This concept sees the supervisor as an integral member of a school faculty, who is in touch with his teachers, who cares about the people he works with, who cares about students, who is able and willing to lead others in self-improvement, who is understanding, and who can communicate about what he sees and believes.

This concept of supervision requires the supervisor to be a model. Whatever the supervisor does serves as a model to the teachers. The supervisor is a living example of how to relate to people. The supervisor cannot escape this demanding role. If the supervisor wants his teachers to improve, then he must show, by example, that it is possible to improve. If he wishes to help teachers become rational decision-makers, then he must be a live demonstration of a rational decision-maker for his teachers to emulate. By his very nonverbal participation with his faculty and by his verbal activity in conferences, for example, the supervisor is communicating powerful messages to his teachers. As a humanistic educator the supervisor can and does instruct his teachers how to relate humanistically tc each other and to their students.

Such an approach to supervision is, indeed, demanding. But the fruit of such a concept is tasteful and satisfying. It leads to long term improvement for the supervisor as well as the teacher. It leads the supervisor to grow and be congruent, that is, to have congruence between action and belief. It leads the supervisor to leading his faculty through example rather than exhortation.

The cornerstone of this book's approach to supervision is observation. The supervisor needs to be able to observe his teachers in action. Knowing what to observe and how to observe is essential in a good supervision program. For this reason, there are several chapters devoted to observing teachers. But, since teaching is a complex, multi-dimensional activity, it is necessary also to provide various perspectives from which to observe. That is to say, just as it is important to observe the climate of the classroom, so, too, is it important to observe cognitive processes, pedagogical inter-action patterns, use of space, and student groupings. No single perspective is sufficient.

Furthermore, once the supervisor observes, he then needs techniques for using the collected data with his teachers. The supervisor needs to know how to communicate his observations to the teachers so that he can help them improve or maintain their current level of achievement. Thus, this book offers two complete chapters and sections of several others on the communication of observations with the intent of helping teachers improve.

In addition to the chapters concerned with observing, there is a complete chapter on teaching strategies. The supervisor needs to know about teaching, as well as observing. The current curriculum reform movement, as well as the efforts to open up the school and provide alternative schools, relies heavily on particular teaching to accomplish its goals. Thus, the supervisor must also know about different strategies of teaching so he may help teachers coordinate their teaching approach with their curriculum content.

Every supervisor knows that he needs many roads to carry his teachers and himself to improvement. He needs approaches consistent with a concept of supervision which focuses on "vision" rather than "super." It is in this light that the two chapters on brainstorming and simulation appear here as effective supervisory strategies.

Finally, there is a chapter focusing on teacher performance objectives. Whether or not the utilization teacher performance objectives become standard practice, there is no doubt that many schools throughout the country already have initiated in-service programs to train supervisors and teachers in the use of these performance objectives. The chapter on performance objectives includes a workshop strategy for helping teachers write their own objectives.

From these comments about the various chapters in this book, it should be obvious that there is a built-in encouragement for you to try out some of the ideas, strategies, and materials presented here. Read the book straight through or read it chapter by chapter according to your preferences. Either way, you will probably find some new idea, strategy, or material. Try it out; use the book to help you help your teachers to improve. Try. Grow.

The emphasis, as you can sense, is on improvement. There is always room to grow and improve in education whether you are in supervision or teaching. No one can stand still. Even to maintain oneself at an acceptable level of competence one must continually try out new ideas because we are in a rapidly changing period. Supervision, as always, is critical to the continuation of quality schooling. A good supervision program demands supervisors who are continually striving to improve by growing with their teachers. Supervisors can and do grow as they internalize various flexible, new approaches in their jobs.

The author recognizes that supervisors in the educational community are both male and female. No inference is intended by the fact that the supervisor is referred to as "he" in this work. This style was chosen for ease in flow rather than the clumsy "he/she" form.

Chapter 2
The Law and Teacher Evaluation:
Utilizing a Value Model

2

The Law and Teacher Evaluation: Utilizing
a Value Model

INTRODUCTION AND OBJECTIVES

The task of the supervisor is to do just that: to super-vise—to over-see. The emphasis should be on the *vision* part—the seeing part—of the task. But the task of supervising continually changes as the legal context shifts and as our insight into teaching grows. For this reason, the supervisor must constantly be alert to subtle yet important changes in what he is to do in our schools. The supervisor must be alert to the demands put on him by new laws and new efforts by teachers and teacher organizations.

This chapter will briefly look at some new state laws related to teacher evaluation and offer a value model for evaluating teachers so as to aid supervisors in their task of helping teachers improve.

At the conclusion of this chapter, the reader should be able to:

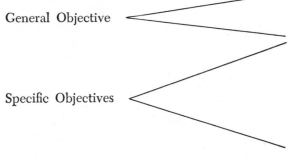

General Objective

1. Understand the structure of a value model for evaluating teachers, in light of the current laws.

Specific Objectives

2. Classify at least 5 teacher activities according to the categories given.
3. Read, with comprehension, 2 examples of the value model applied to teachers.
4. Know how to use the value model with his teachers.

THE NEW LAWS AND THEIR EFFECT

Whether they enjoy it or not, prefer it or not, or are competent at it or not, supervisors have the assignment of evaluating the teachers in their charge. Supervisors then have the further task of recommending to their local boards of education through their superintendent, the head supervisor, that the teacher be rehired, be transferred to another position within the school system, or not be reengaged. This is the case across the country and has been so for a long time.

What is new are the recent laws and court decisions that require supervisors to change certain aspects of their task. For example, in New York the legislature passed the "Fair Dismissal" Act effective July 1, 1972. This law provides, among other items, that a probationary (that is, non-tenured) teacher who is not reengaged may "request in writing that he be furnished with a written statement giving the reasons for such recommendation and within seven days thereafter such written statement shall be furnished." In short, the New York law requires supervisors, when challenged, to show in writing good reasons for not reengaging a non-tenured teacher.

In California the legislature passed the Stull Act in July, 1971. This law focuses on teacher evaluation and includes, among others, the stipulations that (1) each school district must establish its own objective system of evaluation of teachers and (2) a written evaluation plus a face-to-face meeting must be used to relay the evaluation to the teacher. The evaluation must include suggestions for improvement.

Surely there are even newer laws in other states which have been enacted since the writing of this chapter. It doesn't matter. The point is clear. New York and California are our two bellwether states. The course for the future appears clear. Supervisors must be ready to offer good reasons, in writing, for their recommendations regarding probationary teachers.

Moreover, in July, 1975 the State of New Jersey enacted a law which requires a supervisor to observe, evaluate, and confer with a nontenure teacher at least three times a year. The supervisor is required in the conference to identify any deficiencies of the teacher, to extend assistance to the teacher for the correction of deficiencies, and to help the teacher to improve professional competence. If a teacher does not receive a contract for the succeeding school year, he may within 15 days "request in writing a statement of the reasons for such nonemployment which shall be given to the teaching staff member in writing within 30 days after the receipt of such request." This New Jersey law goes beyond the New York and California laws and is quite significant for supervisors.

In June, 1974 the Supreme Court of New Jersey decided that nontenured teachers were entitled to reasons from the Board of Education of the school district as to why they were not reengaged. In this decision, popularly known as The Donaldson Decision since Mary C. Donaldson of North Wildwood, New Jersey, was the plaintiff, the court made several important related points: (1) that teachers are professionals who, when they ask, should be told why they are not being reengaged; (2) that if a teacher requests an informal hearing with the Board of Education, the board should grant the request; and (3) that the court is convinced that the process of furnishing reasons will strengthen rather than impair the tenure system. In its decision the New Jersey Supreme Court cited other related cases decided in the federal and state courts.

The language of the New Jersey Supreme Court in the Donaldson decision is clear, strong, and precise. Because of this the pertinent lines deserve attention here. "It appears evident to us that on balance the arguments supporting the teacher's request for a statement of reasons overwhelm any arguments to the contrary. The teacher is a professional who has spent years in the course of attaining the necessary education and training. When he is engaged as a teacher, he is fully aware that he is serving a probationary period and may or may not ultimately attain tenure. If he is not re-engaged and tenure is thus precluded, he is surely interested in knowing why and every human consideration along with all thoughts of elemental fairness and justice suggest that, when he asks, he be told why."

These new laws and court decisions do not create a "whole new ball game" for a supervisory program. Competent supervisors have always shown good reasons when recommending that teachers be rehired, transferred, or dismissed. They have always helped teachers improve. What these laws and court decisions do is require supervisors to be more judicious, more careful, more sure of their data, more precise, more helping. Now, this is significant because many supervisors realize that their previous procedures for gathering data, as well as the kind of data and improvement suggestions they have used, will simply not hold up in a court of law under the sharp questioning tactics of the plaintiff's lawyer. No supervisor looks forward to losing face and being reversed by court action.

A VALUE MODEL FOR TEACHER EVALUATION

Thus the immediate effect of the new Fair Dismissal Law, the Stull Act, and the recent court decisions is to have supervisors tighten up their evaluative procedures. This means that supervisors must begin by sharpening the evidence they use in their evaluation of teachers. This is quite natural and logical. This further means that supervisors must carefully observe their teachers because observations are the prime data from which supervisors will establish evidence. This, too, is quite natural and logical as shown by the model we use in evaluation (see Figure 2-1).

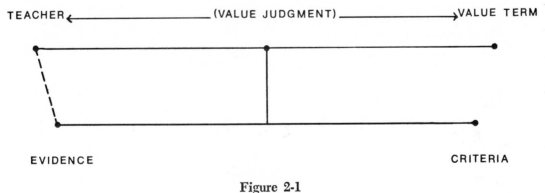

Figure 2-1
Value Model for Teacher Evaluation

There are five main elements in this evaluation model: (1) The Teacher to be evaluated; (2) The Value Term we use (that is, desirable, good, and so forth); (3) The Value Judgment; (4) Evidence; and (5) Criteria. The figure shows that, on the basis of the four other elements, the supervisor makes a Value Judgment about the teacher. The key is to recognize that Evidence and Criteria support the Value Judgment, that fifth element which grows out of the interaction of the other parts of the model. What is more, the Evidence must relate directly to the given Teacher and the Criteria used. The model calls for evidence not just facts. Evidence is more than facts; it is pertinent facts that connect the teacher to the criteria. Evidence is that set of facts which will withstand challenging criticism and, if necessary, be admitted in court as pertinent to the case at hand.

EVIDENCE FOR EVALUATING TEACHERS

This last statement about evidence in court comes not as a scare tactic. It simply comes as a recognition that more and more teachers are going to court to contest decisions about them. Teachers have stronger organizations now than in the past. Furthermore, these teacher organizations have leaders and legal staffs who are willing to back their members who feel professionally and legally injured.

Now, as he uses this evaluation model, the supervisor will surely gather facts about the teacher from students he talks with. He will gather facts about the teacher from concerned parents he confers with personally or on the telephone. He will gather facts by reading reports submitted by the teacher. He will gather facts from other teachers. But, all these facts may not constitute much, if any *evidence*, since they are second hand facts. They are word-of-mouth facts, which are easily challenged and denied the high status of evidence. Clearly, then, the supervisor must gather other kinds of facts than these.

For *evidence*, the supervisor must turn to his own observations of the teacher. He will observe the teacher at faculty meetings, in the faculty room, at school affairs, in the halls, and in the conferences with him. But the observations made at these times, precise as they may be, *will not suffice* as evidence either. The supervisor must make other, *essential* observations when the teacher is teaching. To fully understand this point we must turn to an examination of activities which teachers perform.

TYPES OF TEACHER ACTIVITIES

Figure 2-2 is a short and typical list of some activities a teacher might perform during the course of a week in school. In this list, we note such activities as attending faculty meetings, chaperoning dances, and patrolling halls. But these are not the essential activities of a teacher, even though he performs them with regularity. These are the "institutional activities" of the teacher. As we look at the other activities in the list we note two groups. One group includes such items as questioning, respecting, evaluating, testing, reinforcing, and encouraging. These are the "strategic activities" of the teacher. The other group includes such items as deducing, concluding, explaining, comparing, defining, and justifying. These are the "logical activities" of the teacher.

1. Questioning
2. Deducing
3. Motivating
4. Chaperoning Dances
5. Concluding
6. Explaining
7. Attending Faculty Meetings
8. Testing
9. Taking Roll
10. Trusting

11. Reinforcing
12. Patrolling Halls
13. Defining
14. Evaluating
15. Comparing
16. Justifying
17. Making Reports
18. Collecting Money
19. Encouraging
20. Respecting

Figure 2-2

Let me clarify the labels of these three categories

1. *Institutional Acts* refer to the way the teacher's job in a school is organized by those in charge.

2. *Strategic Acts* refer to the teacher's plans and his ways of directing students during teaching.

3. *Logical Acts* refer to the element of thinking and reasoning about the topic at hand.

When we group the same 20 activities listed in Figure 2-2, the list changes, as shown in Figure 2-3.

Logical Acts	*Strategic Acts*	*Institutional Acts*
1. Deducing	1. Questioning	1. Chaperoning Dances
2. Concluding	2. Motivating	2. Attending Faculty Meetings
3. Explaining	3. Respecting	3. Taking Roll
4. Comparing	4. Evaluating	4. Patrolling Halls
5. Defining	5. Testing	5. Collecting Money
6. Justifying	6. Reinforcing	6. Making Reports
	7. Encouraging	
	8. Trusting	

Figure 2-3

You can try adding some other activities, yourself, to this list by keeping in mind the three definitions of the categories given and the activities already listed in them. Try these activities in addition to any of your own:

21. Giving Opinions on Topic
22. Planning Lessons
23. Generalizing Ideas
24. Maintaining Rapport
25. Conferring with Supervisor
26. Counseling Students

Compare your classifications with the ones below:

21. Giving Opinions on Topic	Logical Acts
22. Planning Lessons	Strategic Acts
23. Generalizing Ideas	Logical Acts
24. Maintaining Rapport	Strategic Acts
25. Conferring with Supervisor	Institutional Acts
26. Counseling Students	Strategic Acts

This three-part classification system is, by no means, error proof. Some items are difficult to classify because the interpretation and context change with the situation. But, it is not the intent here to achieve a 100% tight way of grouping a teacher's activities. Rather, the attempt is to offer an insightful way to look at what a teacher does. This way of grouping leads us to seek balanced, strong evidence about teachers, as we shall see later in this chapter and book.

This point on balanced, strong evidence is important. Although the logical and strategic acts are different, both are essential in teaching. Professor Thomas F. Green of Syracuse University rightly points out that it is possible for a teacher to perform only the activities in the strategic and logical groups and not those in the institutional group, and still, we would say that he is teaching. If he performs none of the items in the strategic and logical groups and only those in the institutional group, we can obviously question if he is a *teacher*. If we have a staff member who only chaperones dances, confers with parents, takes roll, and collects money, we can surely say, "He may be a professional aide or a parent helper but he isn't a *teacher*." On the other hand, it is possible, although not desirable, to teach in a classroom and not personally perform any of the activities listed under institutional acts. Institutional acts are necessary for operating a school. But for classroom teaching only logical acts and strategic acts are necessary.

THREE LOOKS AT ESSENTIAL TEACHER ACTIVITIES

To amplify this point regarding the essential dimensions of teaching, let us turn to three types of people: the student, the teacher, and the judge. If you ask a student what important things he expects his teacher to do, he will put the following items very high on his list: "explains things," "encourages me to do well," and "doesn't ridicule or reject me." Naturally, these activities are essential in teaching. The student knows it even though he is unsophisticated in the use of educational jargon. And there is research evidence as well as personal anecdotes to support this claim. (See my data in the *Research Bulletin*, Vol. 11, No. 2, Winter, 1966, pp. 18–24 and *The Teacher-Pupil Relationship*, a monograph published through the Rutgers University Research Council, 1968.) Note what groups of activities these items belong to.

If you ask a teacher what is important, he might well indicate his preferences by stating what he does *not* want to do. He might say, "The first thing I'd like to drop is the constant collecting of money for the Red Cross, the PTA, UNICEF, or whatever. I feel like a bookkeeper. If I could drop that stuff and maybe some lunchroom duties, I could get on with the show. Let the teachers teach and let someone else be bookkeeper and policeman." It is precisely because of such criticisms that many schools have hired para-professionals or teacher aides. These new staff people free the teacher from the unessential, institutional activities so that he may spend more time performing *professional* activities. But note what these professional activities are, that is, what the teacher implicitly prefers to do in contrast to what he prefers to eliminate. Once again, we are left with activities from our second and third groups, the logical and strategic acts.

If you ask a judge what important things a teacher does, he will most likely answer similarly. Let us suppose a principal named Sam Smith comes before a judge as a defendant because he recommended that Jonathan Jones be dismissed as a teacher in his school. Jonathan Jones has brought suit against Smith, claiming that he is, indeed, a good teacher and deserves to be retained. Jones's lawyer may question Sam Smith as follows:

Lawyer: Mr. Smith, tell us your evaluation of Jonathan Jones as lunch room supervisor.

Principal: Poor, worst in the whole faculty. Kids are always noisy in the lunch room.

Lawyer: And as a participant in faculty meetings?

Principal: Quiet. Doesn't participate much. He's hardly what you would call the majority leader of the faculty floor. So I'd rate him as below average for his lack of contribution.

Lawyer: And as a hall patrolman, PTA member, budget proposer for supplies?

Principal: All very low. He even requested $10,000 for supplies over the limit and that's $11,000 more than any other teacher. He'd run us into the red buying supplies for his classroom.

Lawyer: Then tell us, Mr. Smith, how you evaluate Jonathan Jones on two items. With students in the classroom is he warm, respectful, and positive?

Principal: Superior.

Lawyer: With students is he clear? Do his students understand him and vice versa?

Principal: Superior. He really teaches his students to think.

Lawyer:	And now just a few facts, Mr. Smith. Which teacher did the students vote the "rookie of the year?"
Principal:	Jones.
Lawyer:	Which class performed and entered more projects in the state contest than any other?
Principal:	Jones's.
Lawyer:	That is all, your Honor. Thank you, Mr. Smith.

It is easy to imagine what a judge might conclude in a case like this. His final statement might go like this:

Judge:	In many respects, the principal found Jones lacking and of poor quality. Jones has not at all protested that he deserved a low rating in hall patrolling, lunch room guarding, budget requesting, and faculty leading. But, the weight of these and the many more items like them is not more than the weight of classroom teaching. The quantity of poor ratings is not sufficient reason for deciding on Jones's quality. Surely it would have been possible to find other people to patrol the halls and guard the lunch room in order to keep Jones at his main task, classroom teaching of our young citizens, for which he achieved the highest rating. After all, this is why we send our youth to school. . . . This court finds Jones's case sound and decides in his favor.

Obviously, these three examples from a student, a teacher, and a judge are a bit oversimplified and extreme. Yet the point in all of this is clear. Certain activities of the teacher are obviously much more important than others. Some are essential, some are not. It behooves the supervisor, then, once he realizes this to concentrate on these essential activities. This, in no way, means that the supervisor has to forget or ignore the institutional acts. For there is no doubt that taking roll, for example, is necessary for a school system to operate. Or, there is no doubt that conferring with supervisors and attending faculty meetings contribute to the overall good functioning of a teacher in a school, which in turn, leads to the teacher's good functioning in the classroom. The point here is that if the supervisor wishes to evaluate the teacher as a classroom teacher, then he must concentrate on the essential activities of *teaching*, the logical acts and the strategic acts.

EXAMPLES OF THE VALUE MODEL IN USE

Now, if a supervisor wishes to observe these essential activities, then he must go to the classroom, for here is where the teacher most often interacts logically and strategically with the students. It is in the classroom where the essential activities of teaching take place. For this reason, the supervisor must gather his prime evidence for evaluating teachers by directly observing in the classroom rather than by any other means. Secondhand, word-of-mouth facts will not do, nor will firsthand facts about nonessentials. Direct classroom observance of the logical and strategic acts yields data, which a supervisor can use as evidence to support a value judgment regarding the quality of a teacher. Firsthand essential data constitute strong evidence, and we shall now turn to the matter of using such data in our value model.

Let us take two examples, one negative and one positive.

a. NEGATIVE JUDGMENT

Let us suppose that the supervisor and teacher have mutually agreed that one criterion for good teaching concerns the interaction patterns in the classroom. That is, in good teaching students will talk to each other by reacting to each other's contributions, will ask questions of the teacher and other students, will respond to their teacher's and classmates' questions, and will offer suggestions about which activities and topics to pursue in class. Now, when the supervisor observes this teacher, he notes the following items: The teacher, in fifteen minutes, asked over 30 questions and the students' sole task was to respond to the teacher's questions. On the second time he observes, the principal notes virtually the same pattern with only a slight change in student responsibility. Let us look just at this aspect in reference to our value model. See Figure 2-4.

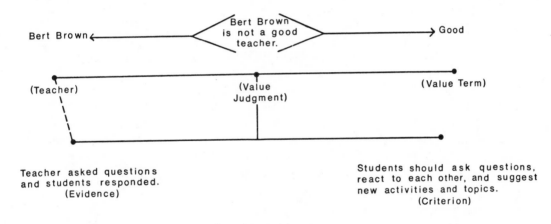

Figure 2-4

Example of the Use of the
Value Model for Teacher Evaluation

We interpret Figure 2-4 in this way: since the evidence does not meet their mutual criterion for good teaching, the supervisor's judgment of Bert Brown is negative. The supervisor evaluates Brown as "not good" in regard to this aspect of teaching. If he has many more instances like this, he will evaluate Bert Brown generally as not good and then he will recommend that Brown not return to his school next year. (For more details, see Chapter 5, *How to Observe and Improve Pedagogical Interaction Patterns.*)

b. POSITIVE JUDGMENT

Let us suppose that the supervisor and teacher have mutually agreed that one criterion for good teaching concerns positive tone in the classroom. That is, in good teaching, the teacher will be warm to the students, will be accepting, will use original and creative ideas, and will be patient. Now, when the supervisor observes this teacher, he notes that the teacher in a 40 minute lesson utilized student ideas, praised students for their contributions, and requested and waited a short while for new suggestions by the students. Let us look just at this aspect in reference to our value model.

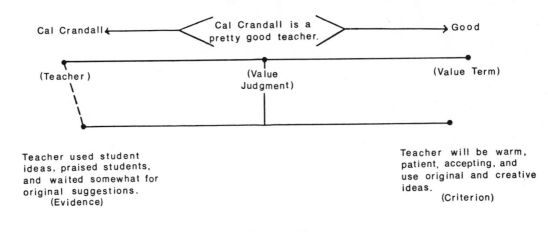

Figure 2-5

Example of the Use of the
Value Model for Teacher Evaluation

We interpret Figure 2-5 in this way. Since the evidence meets their mutual criterion for good teaching, the supervisor's judgment of Cal Crandall is positive. The supervisor evaluates Crandall as "pretty good" in regard to this aspect of teaching. He did not judge Crandall as "good" because Crandall was a bit lacking in patience. Nevertheless, "pretty good" is a positive judgment. If the supervisor has many more instances like this and even gets some improvement, he will evaluate Cal Crandall generally as good and then he will recommend that Crandall return to his school next year. (For more details on classroom climate see Chapter 5, *How to Observe and Improve Classroom Climate*.)

CRITERIA FOR EVALUATING TEACHERS

The key to this value model is deciding upon the criteria for good teaching, or excellent teaching, or what have you, and then gathering evidence specifically connecting these criteria with the teaching. There is no single list which all educators accept as the "standard authority" on good teaching. The supervisor with his colleagues must draw up the criteria he will use. They must consider if each accepted criterion applies to all the teachers. If not, then they must decide which criteria apply to which teachers. For example, let us return to Figure 2-4 and Figure 2-5. Do these two criteria apply to all teachers? Should all teachers seek to have students ask questions and suggest new activities? Or, does this criterion apply to just elementary school teachers? Should all teachers be warm and use creative ideas? Or, does this criterion only apply to the art teacher for the middle school?

Try these criteria for good teaching:

To whom do these apply?

1. The teacher should be dynamic. That is, he should be energetic, outgoing, and assertive.

2. The teacher should ask creative questions. That is, he should ask questions which require the students to be creative in responding. For example, what would we eat if cows did not exist?

3. The teacher should not ridicule or humiliate the students, but accept them as they are positively, and move from there.

4. The teacher should strive to instill proper and effective communication skills in the students.

5. The teacher should exemplify the social values of our nation.

6. The teacher should be a model of the rational decision-maker and problem-solver during his lessons.

Suppose that you accept these 6 criteria.

What evidence would you gather to fit into the model so that you could make a supportable value judgment on the teacher to whom these criteria apply?

The answers to questions on criteria are tough to offer. For the question, "to whom do the criteria apply," there are no right or wrong answers. The answer depends on your judgment made in collaboration with your faculty, your fellow supervisors, and perhaps with your board of education. The answer to the question, "what evidence exists," depends in some measure on the determination of the first answer. For this reason, it is impossible to determine ahead of time just whether or not the evidence is appropriate to the criterion. But, try out your answers with some colleagues to assess their applicability to the criteria.

If the supervisor will keep in mind this model and the nature of the various types of teacher activities, then he need not worry about establishing a good enough case to meet the standards of "fair dismissal laws" wherever they apply. This value model is a rational approach to evaluation. It is congruent with our concept of law, which is a rational set of rules by which we govern ourselves democratically.

One final point remains. A supervisor ought not to infer from the above reasoning that the only, or even most important, purpose of observing a teacher is to gather evidence in order to evaluate. If he restricts observing to the evaluative purpose, the supervisor will soon find himself in an undesirable position. No teacher likes to have a supervisor observe him solely to build up a case against him. If the teacher knows that the supervisor will only use what he observes as evidence connected with evaluation, then he will limit his activities with the students and his interaction with the supervisor. In short, the teacher will teach with a distorted aim just to achieve a high rating, and the supervisor will soon achieve the status of the ogre rather than col-league.

The supervisor should be alert to other reasons for observing his teachers. He should be aware of *what to observe* and *how to observe* in addition to *why to observe*. We shall treat these matters in more detail in the next chapter.

APPLICATION OF THE VALUE MODEL

The supervisor can use this value model with his teachers in several different, but related, ways. Once the supervisor has this model in mind, he will be able to make sense of many items, which previously appeared unrelated. What is more, the super-visor can help teachers relate the various elements of evaluation to each other.

1. The supervisor should explain the model in its general form to his teachers. This will show teachers what goes into the evaluating procedure. At the same time, the supervisor should present the two examples so that teachers can see the value model in operation.

2. The supervisor should work with teachers in setting forth their criteria for *good teaching*. The supervisor can set forth his criteria, the teachers theirs, and together they can work towards a set of mutually determined criteria for good teaching.

3. When the supervisor and teacher have mutually determined some criteria for good teaching, then they should mutually answer the question: "To whom does each criterion apply?"

4. The supervisor and teachers should then mutually determine, in general, the kind of evidence which will satisfy the criterion. That is, what evidence will serve to support a positive value judgment. Similarly, the supervisor and teacher should mutually determine what in general would support a negative judgment. This evidence should not be only the lack of positive evidence but also activities which run counter to the criterion.

5. The supervisor and teachers might also try Steps 2, 3, and 4 with *excellent teaching* and *poor teaching*.

An effective way to focus on applying the value model is to use the form shown on the next pages. The form asks several basic questions about good teaching which will help teachers and supervisors in their discussions. A blank form (Figure 2-6) follows and a completed one (Figure 2-7) follows it to serve as a sample guide.

Supervisor _____   Date _____

Teachers _____

Criteria for Good Teaching

1. Criterion:

2. To whom does this criterion apply?

3. General evidence to support a positive judgment, such as:

4. General evidence to support a negative judgment, such as:

5. Evidence to be gathered by:

Figure 2-6

Criteria for Good Teacher Form—Blank Form

Supervisor _P. Chafey_   Date _10/16/_

Teachers _All Teachers in Wing A_

Criteria for Good Teaching

1. Criterion: _On substantive topics in language arts the teacher will actively encourage students to ask questions of each other so as to stimulate peer learning._

2. To whom does this criterion apply? _Everyone in Wing A._

3. General evidence to support a positive judgment, such as:

   A. _Student presents a project & leads discussion on it._
   B. _Student groups finish an open-ended story, share their endings, and explain them on request._

4. General evidence to support a negative judgment, such as:

   A. _Traditional lesson of teacher questions and student answers_
   B. _Lessons which stick to workbooks_
   C. _No student projects_

5. Evidence to be gathered by: _Teacher self-assessment each week plus supervisor during fortnightly observation._

Figure 2-7

Criteria for Good Teaching Form—Completed Form

Chapter 3

Observing the Classroom Teacher

3

Observing the Classroom Teacher

INTRODUCTION AND OBJECTIVES

Just as listening (see Chapter 10) is all too often forgotten as a communication skill so, too, is observing a neglected skill in our professional and non-professional lives. To observe is much more than mere seeing. Observing involves the intentional and methodical viewing of the teacher and students. Observing involves planned, careful, focused, and active attention by the observer. Observing involves all the senses and not just sight or hearing. As pointed out in the previous chapter, observing is a critical task of the supervisor.

This chapter, then, will devote itself to setting the stage for the following chapters by treating the *why, what,* and *how* of observing as well as some suggestions on general techniques.

At the conclusion of this chapter the reader should be able to:

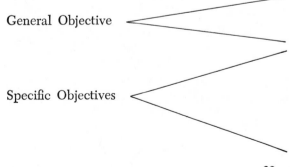

General Objective

1. Understand the nature and importance of classroom observing in the supervision of teachers.

Specific Objectives

2. Give at least three reasons for classroom observations.

3. Identify the essential aspects to observe in the classroom.

4. List two to four issues involved in the nature of observing.

WHY OBSERVE?

There are several reasons for observing teaching in the classroom. First and foremost is the purpose of helping teachers by providing precise and systematic feedback. When you observe a teacher, you gather information to feed back to him so he can know what his performance is as seen by another person. And feedback is essential to the teacher (see Chapter 9). The supervisor, who does not observe the teacher, simply cannot provide the comprehensive and precise feedback which is necessary for a fruitful feedback session.

Second, observing offers you the opportunity to assess the changes a teacher makes over time. Once you feed back data which you intend to serve as an impetus to the teacher's adjustment of future performances, you then need to observe the classroom to see those changes made. You cannot assume that the teacher has changed just because you have talked about changing.

Third, when you observe, you can gather the key evidence you need for teacher evaluation. This evidence is required by the evaluation presented in the preceding chapter. Furthermore, not only *can* you gather this evidence by observing the teacher in the classroom, but you can *only* gather this strong evidence you need by observing. Other means of gathering information simply do not provide the kind of evidence required today in evaluation procedures.

Fourth, when you observe the teacher in the classroom, you reflect your concern for the teacher and the students. You demonstrate an interest in the teacher and the students. Your action conveys the message, "I care and I want to know firsthand what is going on in this classroom which is in my charge." A teacher, who is not observed, soon gets the feeling that nobody feels what he is doing is important. He thinks no one is interested enough in him and his students to come to see them. The teacher who is not observed and feels the lack of interest does not have high morale. A teacher who feels that you care about what he is doing in his classroom is able to convey a feeling of concern to his students.

These four reasons are strong. They support classroom observing which, in turn, is the basis of a sound supervision program. Which supervisor does not wish to implement a sound supervision program?

WHAT TO OBSERVE

The observer cannot just observe. He needs to know what to observe. He must choose from among the many activities and objects in the classroom. The classroom is a complex and active place even when there appears to be little physical movement by the teacher and students. Much is going on at all times. It is important, obviously, that the observer focus on critical aspects. Here we return to the essential activities identified in the previous chapter, the logical and strategic acts of teaching. If you will focus on observing these logical and strategic acts in contrast to such items as teacher dress and classroom window neatness, for example, then you will be on the correct path.

HOW TO OBSERVE

Once we have established what to observe, we must now turn to the answer to another basic question: "How do you observe these essential activities of teaching?" To answer this question, we must examine again what it means to observe. Observing is much more than mere seeing. Observing involves the intentional and methodical viewing of the teacher and students. Observing involves planned, careful, focused, and active attention by the observer. Observing involves all the senses and not just sight or hearing.

From this concept of observing, it is quite clear that the observer must be selective. According to one philosopher, "Each observer or recorder is restricted to some fragment of what is going on. The best we attain is some indication of what is outwardly visible from a single point of view for a limited time" (*The Meaning of Human History* by Morris R. Cohen, page 24). This means that the observer must explicitly recognize the need to be selective and select the critical aspects of teaching to focus on. Furthermore, the teacher, who is observed, must recognize that the subsequent feedback is necessarily selective, too.

Being selective involves taking a "point of view," and the easiest way to take one is to choose an *observational instrument* from among the many our educational researchers have developed. An instrument has a built-in framework, a point of view or vantage point, as well as a set of rules for systematically observing and organizing data. In addition to guiding the observer in selecting what to observe, an observational instrument yields reliable and specific data which form the basis of helpful feedback.

The use of specific, objective data is particularly important. Since the data are specific and objective, the teacher is more willing and ready to accept them than he would some general opinion by the observer. The instrument and the data offer the observer a guide in giving feedback and in evaluating so as not to focus only on the areas in which the teacher is deficient. The observer can put the teacher's activities into perspective via data from an observational instrument.

In the five chapters which follow, we are presenting several instruments which offer a balanced approach. One instrument focuses on the social-emotional climate (tone) of the classroom; one instrument focuses on the pedagogical interaction patterns; one instrument focuses on cognitive processes; and a cluster of three instruments focuses on the use of space and student groupings. A fifth chapter focuses on strategies of teaching and how to identify them but does not offer a specific instrument. As you can see, these chapters provide a balanced, clear, and easy way to observe the logical and strategic acts of teaching.

The first step with these instruments is to read the chapter devoted to the point of view you wish to begin with. Because you cannot choose all points of view at the same time, you must be selective here, too. The best way may be to read them in the order presented. Next, practice using the instruments and ideas according to the suggested steps listed for each one.

When you use the instrument in the classroom, it is most important that you clearly notify the teacher about which one you are using. You can do this either before or after your observation. The teacher and you can communicate effectively when you know each other's point of view. Two people can understand each other when each knows how the other views the situation. When both parties know what is being observed via a particular instrument, then they can communicate effectively and have helpful feedback based on the known point of view.

As you observe, whether for social climate, pedagogical patterns, cognitive processes, spacing, grouping, or strategies, you will find it helpful to take written notes. At times taking written notes may be a bit awkward, so you will not want to take notes in addition to the tallies you keep on the observation forms you use. In any case, you should be taking as precise as possible mental notes, which you can use in your subsequent supervisory reports.

At times, you may even not wish to use the observation forms to record your observations on the spot. If so, then you should be most familiar with the categories and key concepts taken from the observation instruments which constitute the point of view you have selected to use. Keep them in mind at all times. You will need to be doubly attentive since you will not have the observation form and the tallying to guide you. It *is* possible to observe in this informal way. You will need to train yourself to do this by practicing it and comparing yourself against the times when you do use the observation forms.

Obviously, you should sit in a place in the room where you do not need to strain your senses. You should be able to see well—that is, see the teacher and the students. You should be able to hear them all well, too.

These are the two senses you will use most. But in some classes you should be sure to position yourself so that you can touch, smell, and even taste, too. For example, in laboratory or shop class you might well wish to touch the materials being used by the teacher and students.

Finally, you are no doubt aware of several problem issues that arise whenever anyone observes in the classroom. Many of these are theoretical problems, which are already solved by the very way the instruments were designed by the researchers who developed them. Therefore, you need not worry about them. Other problems are those which will be unique to your particular situation. By following the suggestions offered here and getting the feel of your own teachers' classrooms you can deal with these problems as they arise easily.

The key is to remember that observing is an essential element in a sound supervision program. It provides the central data for feedback and evaluation procedures. It provides baseline data for a long term improvement program of teachers. And improvement of teaching, according to the research, is the most important contribution of the supervisor as identified by classroom teachers. With practice and effort you can establish a sound supervision program founded on classroom observation.

Chapter 4

How to Observe and Improve Classroom Climate

4

How to Observe and Improve
Classroom Climate

INTRODUCTION AND OBJECTIVES

Because of their broader perspective and, in general, their added experience, supervisors are rightly concerned with a positive classroom climate. The climate, or tone, or atmosphere of the classroom is an element which promotes or inhibits the teaching and learning situation in the classroom. Obviously then, one important task of the supervisor is to be able to assess classroom climate and, when necessary, help teachers improve it.

This chapter will devote itself to presenting a simple but highly effective instrument for measuring classroom climate and to suggesting ways for the supervisor to use the suggested procedure.

At the conclusion of this chapter the reader should be able to:

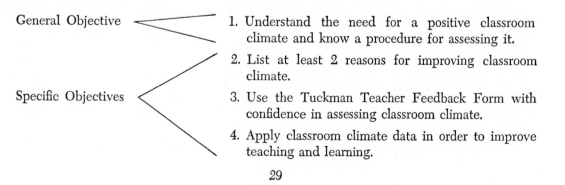

General Objective

1. Understand the need for a positive classroom climate and know a procedure for assessing it.

2. List at least 2 reasons for improving classroom climate.

Specific Objectives

3. Use the Tuckman Teacher Feedback Form with confidence in assessing classroom climate.

4. Apply classroom climate data in order to improve teaching and learning.

ADVANTAGES OF POSITIVE CLIMATE

Concerned educators have been sensitive to classroom climate for hundreds of years. Famous educators, like Locke, Comenius, and Froebel, all urged teachers to improve the atmosphere of the classroom. However, it is only in the last forty years that we have had some empirical data on the effect of different classroom climates on teachers and students. It is only within the last 15 years that supervisors have had available to them instruments which they can use in their daily jobs in the school.

It is possible to sum up all the research on classroom climate in one sentence and it can easily serve as the overall reason for a positive climate: Education conducted in an atmosphere which is positive is desirable—teachers teach better, students learn more, and attitudes toward school improve as climate moves from negative to positive.

Classroom climate refers to overall attitudes the teacher and students have toward each other. Climate is the generalized tone that predominates in the classroom despite any individual differences among particular students. This climate grows out of the interaction between teacher and students as well as the interaction students have among themselves. A climate develops out of the many specific interactions which constitute common activities. Although it may not be explicitly discussed, the classroom climate develops as an expression of the attitudes the teacher and students have towards each other. The climate is obviously intangible but an observer can sense it by perceiving the talk and behavior of the classroom.

Once it is established, classroom climate definitely influences the teacher and the students. A positive climate encourages students to learn. It fosters: (1) further helpful interaction among students; (2) clarifying experiences between teacher and students; (3) a pervasive momentum to carry classroom activities forward; (4) understanding between the teacher and students; (5) respect between people; and (6) further learning of the material at hand.

THE TEACHER AS CLIMATE SETTER

As we talk about classroom climate a certain cluster of words reappears over and over. The cluster centers around such key ideas as teacher influence, emotional distance, domination, integration, democracy, and authoritarianism. These ideas or concepts form the basis of virtually all of the research on climate. The essential thing about this cluster is the recognition that the teacher sets the climate of the classroom. By virtue of his position, the teacher has the power to set the climate he chooses. Though some educators would like to claim innocence with regard to climate, research data time and time again shows the teacher to be responsible for setting the atmosphere of the classroom.

Educational researchers owe a debt to the group in the 1930's headed by Kurt Lewin at the University of Iowa who studied the effects of *authoritarian, democratic,* and *laissez-faire* leaders on members of various youth clubs. In applying the work of Lewin to the classroom, educators have concentrated on two main patterns of teacher leadership, the democratic or integrative pattern and the authoritarian or dominative pattern.

We can synthesize these two patterns of teacher behavior as in Figure 4-1:

Integrative Pattern	*Dominative Pattern*
1. Supports, clarifies, accepts student ideas	1. Expresses and imposes own ideas for students to learn
2. Praises, encourages students	2. Rejects, criticizes, ignores students
3. Facilitates student participation in classroom decision making	3. Controls decisions and gives directions
4. Open and warm	4. Closed and cold
5. Close to students	5. Distant, aloof from students

Figure 4-1

The problem with such broad patterns is the difficulty in assessing classroom climate. We need to know what the climate is of a teacher's classroom before we can legitimately work with the teacher in changing it. But too many instruments used by researchers cannot easily be applied by the supervisor in his daily job. These instruments are too complicated to learn and use with special, lengthy training. Recently Professor Bruce Tuckman of Rutgers University has published a simple but valid and reliable instrument, which on-the-job supervisors can learn and use effectively.

AN EFFECTIVE, EASILY USED INSTRUMENT FOR ASSESSING CLASSROOM CLIMATE

What follows is an observational instrument that we have successfully used in research and school supervision.

The Tuckman Teacher Feedback Form

A. The Instrument

B. Strategy for using this instrument for assessing classroom climate

C. Explanation of the instrument

D. Suggestions and comments

a. THE INSTRUMENT

The Tuckman Teacher Feedback Form follows on the next page. Look it over now.

b. STEP BY STEP PROCEDURE FOR USING THE TUCKMAN TEACHER FEEDBACK FORM TO OBSERVE CLASSROOM CLIMATE

(Before we begin let us be clear that this strategy is just for observing climate. Many supervisors will wish strategies for improving classroom climate based on this instrument. They should see the section on *How to Use the Tuckman Teacher Feedback Form to Improve Classroom Climate* later in this chapter.)

Person Observed _____   Observer _____

Date: _____   Time: _____

Tuckman Teacher Feedback Form

1.	ORIGINAL	__:	__:	__:	__:	__:	__:	__:	CONVENTIONAL
2.	PATIENT	__:	__:	__:	__:	__:	__:	__:	IMPATIENT
3.	COLD	__:	__:	__:	__:	__:	__:	__:	WARM
4.	HOSTILE	__:	__:	__:	__:	__:	__:	__:	AMIABLE
5.	CREATIVE	__:	__:	__:	__:	__:	__:	__:	ROUTINIZED
6.	INHIBITED	__:	__:	__:	__:	__:	__:	__·	UNINHIBITED
7.	ICONOCLASTIC	__:	__:	__:	__:	__:	__:	__:	RITUALISTIC
8.	GENTLE	__:	__:	__:	__:	__:	__:	__:	HARSH
9.	UNFAIR	__:	__:	__:	__:	__:	__:	__:	FAIR
10.	CAPRICIOUS	__:	__:	__:	__:	__:	__:	__:	PURPOSEFUL
11.	CAUTIOUS	__:	__:	__:	__:	__:	__:	__:	EXPERIMENTING
12.	DISORGANIZED	__:	__:	__:	__:	__:	__:	__:	ORGANIZED
13.	UNFRIENDLY	__:	__:	__:	__:	__:	__:	__:	SOCIABLE
14.	RESOURCEFUL	__:	__:	__:	__:	__:	__:	__:	UNCERTAIN
15.	RESERVED	__:	__:	__:	__:	__:	__:	__:	OUTSPOKEN
16.	IMAGINATIVE	__:	__:	__:	__:	__:	__:	__:	EXACTING
17.	ERRATIC	__:	__:	__:	__:	__:	__:	__:	SYSTEMATIC
18.	AGGRESSIVE	__:	__:	__:	__:	__:	__:	__:	PASSIVE
19.	ACCEPTING (People)	__:	__:	__:	__:	__:	__:	__:	CRITICAL
20.	QUIET	__:	__:	__:	__:	__:	__:	__:	BUBBLY
21.	OUTGOING	__:	__:	__:	__:	__:	__:	__:	WITHDRAWN
22.	IN CONTROL	__:	__:	__:	__:	__:	__:	__:	ON THE RUN
23.	FLIGHTY	__:	__:	__:	__:	__:	__:	__:	CONSCIENTIOUS
24.	DOMINANT	__:	__:	__:	__:	__:	__:	__:	SUBMISSIVE
25.	OBSERVANT	__:	__:	__:	__:	__:	__:	__:	PREOCCUPIED
26.	INTROVERTED	__:	__:	__:	__:	__:	__:	__:	EXTROVERTED
27.	ASSERTIVE	__:	__:	__:	__:	__:	__:	__:	SOFT-SPOKEN
28.	TIMID	__:	__:	__:	__:	__:	__:	__:	ADVENTUROUS

Figure 4-2
Tuckman Teacher Feedback Form—Blank

Phase I: Using the Tuckman Form

> Step 1. Read over the 28 pairs of adjectives so that you are familiar with all of them. (See Figure 4-2)

> Step 2. Schedule an observation period with the teacher. Plan for a period of about 40–45 minutes. Use a shorter period only if it constitutes an entire lesson.

> Step 3. Observe the classroom, keeping in mind the 28 pairs of adjectives as best you can.

> Step 4. Mark the teacher on the 28 items by placing an X on one of the seven dashes between each pair of adjectives. For example, take the first pair

Original —: —: —: —: —: —: —: Conventional

If you feel that the adjective *original* very accurately describes the teacher, place an X on the dash right next to *original,* as shown below.

Original X: —: —: —: —: —: —: Conventional

If you feel that the adjective *conventional* very accurately describes the teacher, place an X on the dash right next to *conventional,* as shown below.

Original —: —: —: —: —: —: X: Conventional

If you feel that the adjective *original* is somewhat descriptive, place an X on the second space from the left; if slightly descriptive, place an X on the third space from the left. If you feel that the adjective *conventional* is somewhat descriptive, place an X on the second space from the right; if slightly descriptive, place an X on the third space from the right.

If you feel that either adjective is equally appropriate (or non-appropriate), place an X on the middle dash.

Mark each pair of the 28 adjectives with one X only. Score every pair.

Phase II: Scoring the Tuckman Form

> Step 1. Above the first set of dashes write the numbers 7-6-5-4-3-2-1. This will give a number value to each of the seven spaces between the 28 pairs of adjectives.

> Step 2. Determine the number value for each pair. Write the value into the formula given on the Summary Sheet, which follows in Figure 4-3.
>
> For example, if you placed an "X" on the second dash next to Original in Pair 1, then write the number 6 on the dash under Pair 1 in the summary formula.

> Step 3. Plug the value for each of the 28 pairs into the summary formula.

> Step 4. Compute the score for each of the 4 dimensions which constitute the Tuckman Teacher Feedback Form by using the summary formula. You now have 4 numbers which give you a highly usable way of describing classroom climate.

Person Observed _____   Observer _____

Date _____   Time _____

Tuckman Teacher Feedback Form—Summary Sheet

A. *Item Scoring Procedure Summary*

1. Place an "X" on one of the seven dashes between each pair of adjectives.

2. Above the first set of dashes on the sheet of 28 items write the numbers 7-6-5-4-3-2-1. This will give a number value to each of the seven spaces between the 28 pairs of adjectives.

3. Determine the number value for the first pair, Original-Conventional. Write it into the formula given below on the appropriate line under Item 1.

   For example, if you place an "x" on the second dash next to "Original" in Item 1, then write the number "6" on the dash under Item 1 in the Summary Formula below.

4. Do the same for each of the 28 items. Plug each value into the formula.

5. Compute the score for each of the four dimensions in the Summary Formula below.

B. *Summary Formula & Score for the Four Dimensions of Classroom Climate*

I. Creativity

$$\text{Item } (1 + 5 + 7 + 16) - (6 + 11 + 28) + 18$$
$$(\_ + \_ + \_ + \_) - (\_ + \_ + \_) + 18 = \_\_\_$$

II. Dynamism (Dominance & Energy)

$$\text{Item } (18 + 21 + 24 + 27) - (15 + 20 + 26) + 18$$
$$(\_ + \_ + \_ + \_) - (\_ + \_ + \_) + 18 = \_\_\_$$

III. Organized Demeanor (Organization & Control)

$$\text{Item } (14 + 22 + 25) - (10 + 12 + 17 + 23) + 26$$
$$(\_ + \_ + \_) - (\_ + \_ + \_ + \_) + 26 = \_\_\_$$

IV. Warmth & Acceptance

$$\text{Item } (2 + 8 + 19) - (3 + 4 + 9 + 13) + 26$$
$$(\_ + \_ + \_) - (\_ + \_ + \_ + \_) + 26 = \_\_\_$$

Figure 4-3
Tuckman Teacher Feedback Form—Summary Sheet

Person Observed __D. Foster__   Observer __P. Chafey__

Date: __5/12/__   Time: __8:45–9:27__

Tuckman Teacher Feedback Form

		7	6	5	4	3	2	1	
1.	ORIGINAL				✓				CONVENTIONAL
2.	PATIENT					✓			IMPATIENT
3.	COLD							✓	WARM
4.	HOSTILE							✓	AMIABLE
5.	CREATIVE				✓				ROUTINIZED
6.	INHIBITED							✓	UNINHIBITED
7.	ICONOCLASTIC				✓				RITUALISTIC
8.	GENTLE		✓						HARSH
9.	UNFAIR						✓		FAIR
10.	CAPRICIOUS						✓		PURPOSEFUL
11.	CAUTIOUS				✓				EXPERIMENTING
12.	DISORGANIZED				✓				ORGANIZED
13.	UNFRIENDLY							✓	SOCIABLE
14.	RESOURCEFUL				✓				UNCERTAIN
15.	RESERVED						✓		OUTSPOKEN
16.	IMAGINATIVE				✓				EXACTING
17.	ERRATIC				✓				SYSTEMATIC
18.	AGGRESSIVE				✓				PASSIVE
19.	ACCEPTING (People)		✓						CRITICAL
20.	QUIET							✓	BUBBLY
21.	OUTGOING	✓							WITHDRAWN
22.	IN CONTROL						✓		ON THE RUN
23.	FLIGHTY						✓		CONSCIENTIOUS
24.	DOMINANT	✓							SUBMISSIVE
25.	OBSERVANT						✓		PREOCCUPIED
26.	INTROVERTED							✓	EXTROVERTED
27.	ASSERTIVE	✓							SOFT-SPOKEN
28.	TIMID					✓			ADVENTUROUS

Tuckman Teacher Feedback Form—Completed

Figure 4-4

Person Observed ___D. Foster___   Observer ___P. Chafey___

Date: ___5/12/___   Time: ___8:45-9:27___

Tuckman Teacher Feedback Form—Summary Sheet

A. *Item Scoring Procedure Summary*

1. Place an "X" on one of the seven dashes between each pair of adjectives.

2. Above the first set of dashes on the sheet of 28 items write the numbers 7-6-5-4-3-2-1. This will give a number value to each of the seven spaces between the 28 pairs of adjectives.

3. Determine the number value for the first pair, Original-Conventional. Write it into the formula given below on the appropriate line under Item 1.
   For example, if you place an "x" on the second dash next to "Original" in Item 1, then write the number "6" on the dash under Item 1 in the Summary Formula below.

4. Do the same for each of the 28 items. Plug each value into the formula.

5. Compute the score for each of the four dimensions in the Summary Formula below.

B. *Summary Formula & Score for the Four Dimensions of Classroom Climate*

I. Creativity

$$\text{Item } (\ 1 + \ 5 + \ 7 + 16) - (\ 6 + 11 + 28) + 18$$
$$(\underline{4} + \underline{4} + \underline{4} + \underline{4}) - (\underline{1} + \underline{4} + \underline{3}) + 18 = \underline{26}$$

II. Dynamism (Dominance & Energy)

$$\text{Item } (18 + 21 + 24 + 27) - (15 + 20 + 26) + 18$$
$$(\underline{4} + \underline{7} + \underline{7} + \underline{7}) - (\underline{2} + \underline{1} + \underline{1}) + 18 = \underline{39}$$

III. Organized Demeanor (Organization & Control)

$$\text{Item } (14 + 22 + 25) - (10 + 12 + 17 + 23) + 26$$
$$(\underline{4} + \underline{3} + \underline{2}) - (\underline{2} + \underline{4} + \underline{4} + \underline{3}) + 26 = \underline{22}$$

IV. Warmth & Acceptance

$$\text{Item } (\ 2 + \ 8 + 19) - (\ 3 + \ 4 + \ 9 + 13) + 26$$
$$(\underline{3} + \underline{6} + \underline{6}) - (\underline{1} + \underline{1} + \underline{2} + \underline{1}) + 26 = \underline{36}$$

Figure 4-5
Tuckman Teacher Feedback Form—Summary Sheet—Completed

36

Figures 4-4 and 4-5 offer examples of a completed Tuckman Teacher Feedback Form and a completed Summary Sheet as a guide in learning how to use this instrument.

c. EXPLANATION OF THE TUCKMAN TEACHER FEEDBACK FORM

As you read through the instrument and the step by step procedure for using it, you no doubt had several questions concerning the make-up and scoring procedure for this Tuckman Teacher Feedback Form. Here are 17 commonly asked Questions and Answers that will help explain the instrument to you for your own sake and also so you are able to explain it to your teachers.

1. *Question:* Who is Tuckman?

   Answer: Bruce Tuckman is a Professor of Education at the Graduate School of Education of Rutgers University, The State University of New Jersey.

2. *Question:* Why did he design this instrument?

   Answer: Tuckman is a psychologist interested in conducting research on teaching, especially on the climate of the classroom. He wanted a simple instrument for his many research projects. In many projects he employs student observers whom he must train efficiently and quickly. He wanted an instrument which did not require a long training session, as most of the other available ones require at least 8 hours of training time.

3. *Question:* What's the idea behind the Tuckman instrument?

   Answer: Tuckman is influenced through his own university professor by the psychologist George Kelly. Kelly holds that each person develops a set of ideas which aids him in anticipating and dealing with the future. As a person deals with the present and future, he draws on his established set of "constructs." He processes incoming information via his unique relation to these constructs. Tuckman also holds that the general kinds of constructs that a teacher uses to construe his behavior can be and will be the ones an observer uses to describe the teacher's behavior in a classroom.

4. *Question:* Why are there *pairs* of adjectives?

   Answer: Each pair of adjectives represents a personal construct. In following Kelly, Tuckman holds that a person's picture of reality can be expressed as a unique, overall position on a set of continuous formed by *pairs of adjectives.* For example, each person positions himself somewhere between "cold" and "warm," "gentle" and "harsh," and other dichotomous pairs of adjectives. No two people have exactly the same overall *set of positions* though on any given dichotomy they may be similarly located. The total set of positions is unique for each person. The set of positions represents a person's unique picture of reality.

5. *Question:* Why are there *28* pairs of these adjectives?

   Answer: Tuckman originally had 65 pairs of adjectives which he believed covered the wide and complex range of ideas held by Kelly and Kelly's disciples. These 65 pairs took into account various aspects of a teacher's role as interpreted through Kelly's ideas. The 65 pairs were reduced to 28 key pairs when data were submitted to a factor analysis statistical procedure. In this way the 28 pairs represent the 65 pairs and are certainly easier to work with.

6. *Question:*   What are these 4 clusters or dimensions found on the Feedback Summary Sheet?

   Answer: These are the 4 clusters which emerged from the factor analysis procedure. That is, the 65 pairs of adjectives clustered together in 4 different ways. Tuckman took the top 7 pairs from each cluster to make up the 28 pairs in the instrument.

7. *Question:*   What does a cluster mean?

   Answer: Cluster (or dimension) here means that, in general, those pairs which constitute a cluster have the same meaning for people in regard to teaching. In using this technique of cluster of factors, Tuckman nicely builds on the classic work by Professors Osgood, Suci, and Tannenbaum (of the University of Illinois) called the *semantic differential.* This semantic differential technique asserts that items that cluster together have the same general meaning for people.

8. *Question:*   How did Tuckman come up with the 4 clusters called creativity, dynamism, organized demeanor, and warmth and acceptance?

   Answer: Tuckman inspected the items making up the cluster and labeled the cluster with appropriate names to give some meaning to these clusters. The 4 labels are to give a shorthand summary of what constitutes the cluster.

9. *Question:*   Why are there "plus" and "minus" numbers in the scoring formula?

   Answer·   Positive poles of some of the adjective pairs appear on the left while positive poles of other pairs appear on the right ends of the continuums. In order to balance this out in the scoring there are plus and minus numbers.

10. *Question:*   Well, why were some positive poles put on the left and some on the right?

    Answer: Tuckman mixed up the positive poles to minimize a bias in responding to the adjective pairs. A person can't simply go down the left or the right to check off everything without careful consideration of each pair of adjectives. This is an accepted measurement technique.

11. *Question:*   Why do the values assigned to the dashes go 7-6-5-4-3-2-1 rather than 1-2-3-4-5-6-7?

    Answer: By going up from right to left, then the value of a cluster goes up as the score goes up. This is common and clear. The other way, a low score would mean a high value. That's confusing and Tuckman avoided it. So Tuckman chose the clear way of making a high score equal a high value.

12. *Question:* Why are 18 and 26 added to the four scoring formulas at the end?

Answer: The 18 and 26 are loading factors. Tuckman determined that by adding 18 to the first two cluster formulas and 26 to the last two cluster formulas he could avoid negative scores. (Negative scores are undesirable because they are confusing to people.) With these loading factors of 18 and 26 the minimum score on any cluster is set at 1.

13. *Question:* Then what's the highest score possible?

Answer: Since the lowest score is 1, the highest score is 43.

14. *Question:* What does the final score mean for each cluster?

Answer: The score means something quite simple: The higher the score on a cluster, the more you observed this in the teacher. For example, if a teacher gets a score of 36 on Creativity, then his behavior is considered more creative than another person's behavior with a score of 25.

15. *Question:* Does each of the 28 pairs of adjectives count or do just the 4 clusters count?

Answer: Each of the 28 adjective pairs does not have meaning independently. The clusters have meaning. In teaching, if we follow Kelly's viewpoint, no one can use 28 independent constructs. In giving meaning to behavior in teaching, we need to use clusters of contructs. Every teacher has some score in each cluster. Teachers only differ in regard to the *degree* their behavior shows in each cluster.

16. *Question:* Does the instrument hold water?

Answer: Yes. The Tuckman Teacher Feedback Form is supported by both the research of Kelly and the research of Osgood, Suci, and Tannenbaum. That is, it's supported on the *psychology* side *and* the *measurement* side. Tuckman reports in his research papers that the instrument is both reliable and valid. On a sample of 31 open classroom teachers, a pair of observers achieved correlation reliabilities ranging from 0.65 to 0.90. In another project, high school students achieved a correlation reliability of 0.91. There are also data that show a high correlation between the Tuckman Teacher Feedback Form and the Student Opinion Questionnaire designed at Western Michigan University.

17. *Question:* Who can use this instrument?

Answer: Anyone who observes the teacher in the classroom: supervisor, trained observer, another teacher, a student.

d. SUGGESTIONS AND COMMENTS

Just a few words need to be added here.

1. This instrument calls for an observing time of 40–45 minutes rightly. Though the observing time may be longer than with other instruments, it is justified for two reasons. (a) Teachers resent a short supervisory visit and are angry when they believe that feedback to them is based on too short a sample of their behavior. There is, therefore, no need to begin your supervisory effort with the teachers in opposition. It is simply better to begin with satisfied teachers. (b) This Tuckman instrument is an "impressionistic" one. It relies on a long period of time to give the supervisor the adequate basis for a reliable impression. So, don't cut short the observation time.

2. Be sure to give your feedback to the teacher soon after you score the Tuckman form. Feedback is meaningful if it occurs soon after the observation. If there is a great lag in time, the teacher and you will forget the many details of the classroom. The teacher will feel that you don't care about his teaching and probably become resentful. Try, therefore, to give your feedback by the next day or so.

WHY USE THE TUCKMAN TEACHER FEEDBACK FORM

There are several excellent reasons for utilizing the Tuckman Teacher Feedback Form. However, it is possible to summarize them all in one short sentence: *It works.*

The specific reasons are as follows:

1. The Tuckman Teacher Feedback Form focuses on 4 essential dimensions of the classroom. Creativity, Dynamism, Organized Demeanor, and Warmth and Acceptance are all worthwhile dimensions to focus on in supervision. Each dimension deserves the separate consideration of all teachers and supervisors who are concerned with effecting a positive climate in the classroom. In short, the Tuckman instrument leads us on the right path because it focuses on essential elements of classroom climate. Furthermore, it provides a manageable, behavioral approach to observing climate.

2. The Tuckman Teacher Feedback Form is easy to learn. The instrument involves no new technical terms to "snow" the user. The language in the instrument is simple, everyday English. The language involved in scoring the observed behavior is also simple, everyday English. There is no complicated statistical procedure to learn in order to understand how the instrument works.

3. The Tuckman Teacher Feedback Form is easy to use. There is no long, drawn out training period nor is there any complex statistical analysis required. The user merely calls on his knowledge of arithmetic to compute the teacher's score. The user adds and subtracts eight numbers only for each of the four dimensions of classroom climate.

4. The Tuckman Teacher Feedback Form is research based. Tuckman has shown that different observers viewing the same teacher can easily establish reliability among themselves. That is to say, different observers generally agree in their scoring of the 4 dimensions. Moreover, the Tuckman instrument correlates with and builds upon other research instruments.

5. The Tuckman Teacher Feedback Form is easy to use with the faculty. The supervisor can easily explain the instrument, use the instrument, and report the data gathered by it. The supervisor can work out with the faculty mutually acceptable ways to employ the instrument in their common endeavor of improving classroom climate.

To such application ideas we now turn our attention.

APPLICATION: HOW TO USE THE TUCKMAN TEACHER FEEDBACK FORM TO IMPROVE CLASSROOM CLIMATE

It is one thing to assess a teacher's classroom climate. It is another thing to help teachers *improve* the climate of their classrooms. The step by step strategy described earlier in the chapter is one for assessing, or describing, climate. Here we shall turn our attention to several *short strategies* for helping teachers move toward a *more positive climate.* You may choose any one or more of these strategies to use with your teachers or you may design your own new ones.

a. Several Short Improvement Strategies

Strategy A—the feedback interaction follows:

Supervisor's Description of Teacher ⟷ Teacher's Self-Preference

Step 1

In Figure 4-6, you will find a slight alteration of the Tuckman Teacher Feedback Form. The same 28 pairs of adjectives appear but this time with a new heading. The changed heading is significant. We now have a form to express *preferences* rather than just a description as before. Ask the *teacher* you will be observing to fill out this form for himself—a *self-preference* statement on classroom climate. (Explain to him only how to fill out the form. That is, reveal to him at this time only what is shown as Step 1 under Item Scoring Procedure on the Summary Sheet in Figure 4-7).

Step 2

Explain the meaning and construction of the Tuckman instrument to the teacher. Then explain Steps 2, 3, 4, and 5 under Item Scoring Procedure on the Summary Sheet in Figure 4-7.

Step 3

Observe this teacher for about 40-45 minutes.

Step 4

Fill out the Tuckman Teacher Feedback Form describing your impressions of this teacher's classroom climate.

Step 5

Give the teacher a copy of your description of his classroom climate.

Name _____ •   Date _____

My Preference for _____

1.	ORIGINAL	__: __: __: __: __: __: __:	CONVENTIONAL
2.	PATIENT	__: __: __: __: __: __: __:	IMPATIENT
3.	COLD	__: __: __: __: __: __: __:	WARM
4.	HOSTILE	__: __: __: __: __: __: __:	AMIABLE
5.	CREATIVE	__: __: __: __: __: __: __:	ROUTINIZED
6.	INHIBITED	__: __: __: __: __: __: __:	UNINHIBITED
7.	ICONOCLASTIC	__: __: __: __: __: __: __:	RITUALISTIC
8.	GENTLE	__: __: __: __: __: __: __:	HARSH
9.	UNFAIR	__: __: __: __: __: __: __:	FAIR
10.	CAPRICIOUS	__: __: __: __: __: __: __:	PURPOSEFUL
11.	CAUTIOUS	__: __: __: __: __: __: __:	EXPERIMENTING
12.	DISORGANIZED	__: __: __: __: __: __: __:	ORGANIZED
13.	UNFRIENDLY	__: __: __: __: __: __: __:	SOCIABLE
14.	RESOURCEFUL	__: __: __: __: __: __: __:	UNCERTAIN
15.	RESERVED	__: __: __: __: __: __: __:	OUTSPOKEN
16.	IMAGINATIVE	__: __: __: __: __: __: __:	EXACTING
17.	ERRATIC	__: __: __: __: __: __: __:	SYSTEMATIC
18.	AGGRESSIVE	__: __: __: __: __: __: __:	PASSIVE
19.	ACCEPTING (People)	__: __: __: __: __: __: __:	CRITICAL
20.	QUIET	__: __: __: __: __: __: __:	BUBBLY
21.	OUTGOING	__: __: __: __: __: __: __:	WITHDRAWN
22.	IN CONTROL	__: __: __: __: __: __: __:	ON THE RUN
23.	FLIGHTY	__: __: __: __: __: __: __:	CONSCIENTIOUS
24.	DOMINANT	__: __: __: __: __: __: __:	SUBMISSIVE
25.	OBSERVANT	__: __: __: __: __: __: __:	PREOCCUPIED
26.	INTROVERTED	__: __: __: __: __: __: __:	EXTROVERTED
27.	ASSERTIVE	__: __: __: __: __: __: __:	SOFT-SPOKEN
28.	TIMID	__: __: __: __: __: __: __:	ADVENTUROUS

Figure 4-6

Tuckman Teacher Feedback Form—Preference Form

Name _____ Date _____

My Preference for _____

A. *Item Scoring Procedure Summary*

1. Place an "X" on one of the seven dashes between each pair of adjectives.

2. Above the first set of dashes on the sheet of 28 items write the numbers 7-6-5-4-3-2-1. This will give a number value to each of the seven spaces between the 28 pairs of adjectives.

3. Determine the number value for the first pair, Original-Conventional. Write it into the formula given below on the appropriate line under Item 1.
For example, if you place an "x" on the second dash next to "Original" in Item 1, then write the number "6" on the dash under Item 1 in the Summary Formula below.

4. Do the same for each of the 28 items. Plug each value into the formula.

5. Compute the score for each of the four dimensions in the Summary Formula below.

B. *Summary Formula & Score for the Four Dimensions of Classroom Climate*

I. Creativity

$$\text{Item } (\ 1 + \ 5 + \ 7 + 16) - (\ 6 + 11 + 28) + 18$$
$$(\_ + \_ + \_ + \_) - (\_ + \_ + \_) + 18 = \_\_\_$$

II. Dynamism (Dominance & Energy)

$$\text{Item } (18 + 21 + 24 + 27) - (15 + 20 + 26) + 18$$
$$(\_ + \_ + \_ + \_) - (\_ + \_ + \_) + 18 = \_\_\_$$

III. Organized Demeanor (Organization & Control)

$$\text{Item } (14 + 22 + 25) - (10 + 12 + 17 + 23) + 26$$
$$(\_ + \_ + \_) - (\_ + \_ + \_ + \_) + 26 = \_\_\_$$

IV. Warmth & Acceptance

$$\text{Item } (\ 2 + \ 8 + 19) - (\ 3 + \ 4 + \ 9 + 13) + 26$$
$$(\_ + \_ + \_) - (\_ + \_ + \_ + \_) + 26 = \_\_\_$$

Figure 4-7
Tuckman Teacher Feedback Form—Summary Sheet—Preference Form

43

Step 6

If the teacher would like to discuss the description and his own preferences with you, by all means confer with him.

Step 7

In 2-4 weeks observe the teacher again for about 40-45 minutes.

Step 8

Fill out the Tuckman Teacher Feedback Form once again describing your impressions of this teacher's classroom climate.

Step 9

Give the teacher a copy of your second impressions.

Step 10

Confer with the teacher about the similarities and contrasts in the two observations.

Strategy B—The feedback interaction follows:

Supervisor's Description of Teacher ⟷ Teacher's Self-Description

Step 1

Schedule an observation visit with the teacher you are supervising.

Step 2

Observe the teacher for about 40-45 minutes.

Step 3

Fill out the Tuckman Teacher Feedback Form describing your impressions of this teacher's classroom climate.

Step 4

Ask the teacher to do the same—to describe himself for those same 40-45 minutes.

Step 5

Confer with the teacher about the similarities and contrasts in the two reports—the teacher as he appeared to you and the teacher as he appeared to himself.

Strategy C—the feedback interaction follows:

Teachers B, C, and D's Description of Teacher A ⟷ Teacher A's Self-Preference

Step 1

(Same as Step 1 in Strategy A) Ask the teachers you supervise to fill out the altered Tuckman form—each teacher expressing *his own self-preferences.*

Step 2

Explain the Tuckman instrument to the teachers.

Step 3

Ask teachers to organize themselves into trios or quartets for observation purposes.

Step 4

Ask each trio or quartet to prepare and submit an inter-teacher observation plan.

Step 5

Have teachers observe each other and share their *descriptions of their colleagues* via the feedback from the Tuckman Teacher Feedback Form.

Step 6

Ask each trio or quartet to report briefly in writing the results of their efforts.

Step 7

Confer with each trio or quartet to review their report.

Strategy D—the feedback interaction follows:

Student's Description of Teacher ⟷ Teacher's Self-Preference

Step 1

(Same as Step 1 in Stategy A) Ask the teacher you are supervising to fill out the altered Tuckman form for himself—a *self-preference* statement on classroom climate.

Step 2

Arrange with the teacher you supervise for his students to be observers.

Step 3

Distribute the Tuckman Teacher Feedback Form to the students. Ask them to fill out the form *describing* their impressions of their teacher.

Step 4

Ask the students to give their descriptions to the teacher.

Step 5

If the teacher wishes, confer with him to discuss the similarities and contrasts between the students' description and his own self-preference statement.

Strategy E—the feedback interaction follows:

Supervisor's Preference for Teacher ⟷ Teacher's Self-Preference

Step 1

Fill out the altered Tuckman form showing *your preferences* for the teacher you are supervising.

Step 2

(Same as Step 1 in Strategy A) Ask the teacher you are supervising to also fill out the form for himself—a self-preference statement.

Step 3

Schedule a conference with the teacher and explain the Tuckman form to him.

Step 4

Compare your preferences for the teacher with his self-preferences. Begin with points of agreement. Keep in mind that there is not a "right" viewpoint but only alternatives.

Figure 4-8 summarizes the 5 short strategies presented above.

b. SUMMARY OF FEEDBACK INTERACTIONS

Strategy A:	Supervisor's Description of Teacher ⟷	Teacher's Self-Preference
Strategy B:	Supervisor's Description of Teacher ⟷	Teacher's Self-Description
Strategy C:	Teachers B, C, & D's Description of Teacher A ⟷	Teacher A's Self-Preference
Strategy D:	Students' Description of Teacher ⟷	Teacher's Self-Preference
Strategy E:	Supervisor's Preference for Teacher ⟷	Teacher's Self-Preference

Figure 4-8
Summary of Feedback Interactions

c. What's the Idea Behind the 5 Improvement Strategies

Perhaps you noticed already that there is an essential common feature to all these 5 improvement strategies. All of these strategies rely on the same factor as motivation for change—dissonance. Dissonance is the discrepancy between a person's perception of or preference about his behavior and his actual behavior. Dissonance can also stem from a person's preference about his behavior and someone else's preference about this person's behavior.

Now, according to Leon Festinger, the noted researcher on dissonance and author of the book *A Theory of Cognitive Dissonance*, dissonance is a motivating force for its own reduction. That is to say, when a person feels dissonant, there is motivation for him to reduce the dissonance. Dissonance is a tension which people seek to reduce or remove once they are aware of it.

Strategy A creates a dissonance between the teacher's behavior (as described by the supervisor) and the teacher's preferred behavior. Strategy C and Strategy D create a similar dissonance between behavior and preference but the behavior is described by fellow teachers and students. Strategy B creates a dissonance between the teacher's behavior as described by the supervisor and the teacher's behavior as seen by himself. Strategy E creates a dissonance between the supervisor's preference and the teacher's preference. In each strategy, the teacher becomes aware of the dissonance when in Step 4 or Step 5, he receives feedback from the supervisor, his fellow teachers, or his students.

These 5 strategies raise dissonance within the teacher simply because virtually all teachers are not now teaching the way they would like to and most teachers are now poor describers of their own behavior. Yet, there is no guarantee that all teachers will feel dissonant. There will be a few rare teachers whose behavior matches their self-preference, or self-description, or their supervisor's preference for them. For these few teachers, these strategies will serve to maintain their rare condition rather than improve it.

Once the teacher feels dissonance, he will seek to remove or reduce it. There are several ways a teacher can do this. For example:

1. He can *reject or blur the incoming data.* By claiming that the data is too general, for example, a teacher can remove the dissonance.

2. He can *change his behavior.* In this way, his behavior becomes consonant with his preferred behavior.

3. He can *change his preference.* In this way his preference becomes consonant with his actual behavior.

Our research shows that when teachers receive *specific feedback* they will change their behavior in order to reduce dissonance. Only when there is high dissonance, do teachers change their self-preferences.

In short, most teachers *will change their behavior* to bring it in line with their preference since they are not greatly dissonant. It may take some effort to change behavior but it is easier for most teachers to change their behavior than their preferences which they have held for a long time as the foundation of their professional lives. And this change is desirable. Experience shows that when there is dissonance between classroom climate behavior and classroom climate preference, the preferred climate is the more positive climate. So, the *change in behavior is to a more positive classroom climate.*

What is significant about these 5 improvement strategies is that the reliance on dissonance as the motivation for change eliminates the need for pressure from the supervisor. The teacher's own dissonance acts on the teacher. The supervisor does not have to "come down hard" on the teacher to bring about change. There is no need for lectures and urgings by you. Teachers already hold a more positive view on classroom climate than they are now implementing. For this reason, you can securely call upon other teachers, as well as students, to give feedback as a way of alerting the teacher to the dissonance between his preferred behavior and his actual behavior.

In one case, Strategy E, there is no observation of the teacher, and hence, no feedback is given about the teacher's actual behavior. Nevertheless, the effect of this strategy is positive because the teacher is sensitized to classroom climate in a concrete manner. No longer is classroom climate an intangible, unexpressible idea. Rather, now classroom climate is expressed in common, non-technical language.

What is more, the teacher now knows your beliefs about classroom climate as a supervisor. He knows your preferences specifically. Since he is no longer in the dark about your preferences and expectations as a supervisor, the teacher can begin with you to meaningfully discuss classroom climate in the school.

d. Taking Some Further Steps

When you use these improvement strategies, many times you will be talking with the teachers about *how* they can change their classroom climate. Some teachers will have ideas about what and how to change. Yet, others will seek your help and advice.

It is advisable to set out only a few suggestions at a time. These few suggestions should be quite specific. Teachers can deal with suggested changes if there are only several at a time. Most teachers can change, provided they are not overwhelmed by a score of ideas which are general in nature. Teachers can effect change by implementing a *few specific activities* which are designed for their particular need at the given time.

An effective way to pinpoint these activities and to keep them brief and specific is to use the form on the following pages. Note that the form directs attention to one of the 4 climate dimensions at a time. This keeps the teacher's attention focused. Besides, our research shows that improvement in one dimension has a generalizing effect for the other three. That is, improvement in one of the 4 climate dimensions leads to improvement in the other 3. Keep in mind that "improvement" does not necessarily mean higher and higher scores since there probably is an optimum level in each dimension. Also, note that the form focuses on positive activities—things to do—but does include without emphasis some negative activities—things not to do. A blank form (Figure 4-9) follows and a completed one (Figure 4-10) follows it to serve as a sample guide.

CONCLUDING REMARKS

You as supervisor can use the Tuckman Teacher Feedback Form as an instrument for assessing climate in your teachers' classrooms. You can employ several short strategies based on the Tuckman instrument to guide your teachers to improve classroom climate. *Teachers can effect change in classroom* climate by implementing activities designed to lead to different behavior on their part as well as on the student's part. *Supervisors can help teachers change* with a focus on feedback and specific positive activities.

Teacher _____ Date _____

Supervisor _____ Class _____

On Classroom Climate

Dimension of Concern: _____

Trying to Change Toward Becoming _____

Some New Activities to Do: _____

    A.

    B.

    C.

    D.

Some Features to Maintain/Increase:

    A.

    B.

    C.

Some Features to Stop/Reduce/Avoid:

    A.

    B.

    C.

Date for Re-Assessment? _____

Who Will Do Re-Assessment? _____

Who Can/Will Help Teacher Change? _____

Figure 4-9
Classroom Climate Evaluation Form—Blank

Teacher **D. Foster**   Date **5/13/**
Supervisor **P. Chafey**   Class **Hum. 1**

On Classroom Climate

Dimension of Concern: _____ *creativity* _____

Trying to Change Toward Becoming _*more able to experiment; lover with the kids; willing to use projects that aren't dull*_

Some New Activities to Do: _____

A. *Poetry corner – students to pin up their poems, others read them – they read aloud if requested to*
B. *Mime plays to be written and acted out by students*
C. *Students create their own sound filmstrips with taped sound*
D.

Some Features to Maintain/Increase:

A. *Weekly panel for screening papers and reproducing some for all students to read*
B. *Students initiate field trip with parents; then released from related class trips*
C. *Monthly featured guest speaker*

Some Features to Stop/Reduce/Avoid:

A. *Stop doing all planning —*
B. *Reduce domination of discussions after films*
C. *Stop worrying that students will take advantage*

Date for Re-Assessment? _____ *6/6* _____

Who Will Do Re-Assessment? _____ *P. Chafey* _____

Who Can/Will Help Teacher Change? _*P. Chafey, Sam R., Ted Burns, John Vincent*_

Figure 4-10
Classroom Climate Evaluation Form—Completed

Chapter 5

How to Observe and Improve Pedagogical Interaction Patterns

5

How To Observe and Improve Pedagogical Interaction Patterns

INTRODUCTION AND OBJECTIVES

Who talks to whom in the classroom has been of interest to educational sociologists for a long time. These sociologists recognize the importance of interaction relationships in a group setting. Supervisors and teachers go beyond this interest and seek to know who talks to whom *when*. That is, we want to know what is the sequence of verbal interaction in the classroom we want to know because the pedagogical pattern that develops indicates the type of teaching occurring.

In this chapter we shall treat the importance of interaction patterns, present a simple instrument for assessing the existing classroom patterns, and then suggest ways of improving these patterns.

At the conclusion of this chapter the reader should be able to:

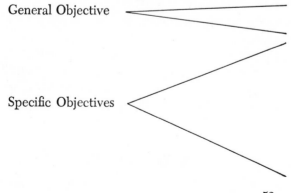

General Objective

1. Understand the significance of various pedagogical interaction patterns.

2. Describe four pedagogical moves that teachers and students make.

Specific Objectives

3. Use the language of the classroom instrument for observing classroom interaction.

4. Apply the language of the classroom instrument for improving the interaction patterns of the classrooms.

CLASSROOM INTERACTION FROM A PEDAGOGICAL PERSPECTIVE

As mentioned earlier, educational sociologists have long been interested in class-room interaction. Their interest stems from their general concern with groups and the relationships group members have among themselves. This is a legitimate concern. For a teacher, however, the sociological perspective cannot suffice. The teacher surely needs sociological data about the groups formed and continually forming in his class-room. But, the teacher—and the supervisor—need other information about the classroom.

The students and the teacher in a classroom form a special kind of group. Their group is not an informal one organized for entertainment purposes or play purposes. The classroom group exists because the teacher is committed to teaching the students. Because of his position as official leader of the classroom, there is no doubt that the teacher is the central figure in the classroom. The teacher accepts that and so do the students. Everyone looks to the teacher as the leader of the classroom group.

For this reason, it is essential to look at the way the teacher interacts with the students. It is significant to gather information about how the teacher uses his teach-ing position to set the *pedagogical* tone of the classroom. The pedagogical tone focuses on the various classroom functions specifically related to teaching. It looks at the functions which are performed by the teacher and student.

To identify the pedagogical functions, it is necessary to recognize several aspects of *teaching as it is.* First, teaching is a *linguistic activity.* Language is essential to teaching. Teachers also communicate non-verbally to students all the time. For exam-ple, they smile, they demonstrate, and they pat students gently as a sign of praise. But along with their non-verbal activity they talk, and they rely on this talk to carry out essential teaching items—clarifying ideas, explaining events, comparing things with others, and making assignments, for example. In short, in every teaching situation, language is at the heart of the communication between teacher and student. This is so even when there is much non-verbal communication.

Second, because teaching is what it is, there is a cluster of activities which uniquely characterizes teaching activity. That is, when we observe this cluster of activities, we know we are in a classroom rather than a store, recreation center, doctor's office, or television studio. This cluster of activities includes the following: making assignments, checking finished assignments, explaining events, praising and criticizing perform-ances, asking questions, answering questions, giving information, announcing topics to be studied, establishing procedures, defining terms, justifying positions, giving direc-tions, demonstrating, and evaluating performances.

Thus, the pedagogical perspective utilizes these ideas mentioned here to ask this question: "Who does what pedagogically in the verbal interaction of the classroom?" This question recognizes that there are different roles being played by the teachers and students as they use language to carry out the cluster of activities which give teaching its unique flavor.

WHY KNOWLEDGE OF CLASSROOM INTERACTION IS IMPORTANT

We seek an answer to the question "who does what pedagogically" because from it we can understand the classroom in a meaningful way. Knowledge about classroom interaction:

1. Indicates the type of involvement students have.

One of the primary tasks of the teacher is to maintain pupil involvement in classroom activities. The student who is involved and actively participating learns more readily than the student who sits on the side passively present, but mentally absent. Everyone, professional and layman alike, recognizes this fundamental fact about teaching. Yet teachers, who are in the act of teaching, may not be aware of just what type of involvement, as manifested in patterns of interaction, their students are experiencing.

Research done at the University of California, Los Angeles (UCLA) showed that a single pedagogical pattern dominated in all but 5 per cent of 150 classrooms in 67 schools. The interaction may be described simply as follows: the teacher asks a question, a student replies correctly in a word or two or short phrase, and the teacher approves the student's response. Other research corroborates this finding. Most teachers follow this type of involvement with regularity even though there is a call for individualization and variety. By knowing the type of interaction going on, the supervisor is in a position to help the teacher with this important task of involvement.

2. Indicates the degree of involvement students have.

Certainly a student who is listening carefully can be said to be actively participating in a given lesson. On the other hand, if a student or group of students seldom or never participates verbally in classroom interaction, then it is highly doubtful that the student is involved. The amount of classroom interaction reflects the amount of involvement. For example, if the teacher does 95% of the talking in the classroom consistently, then it is fair to infer that the students are not very involved at all. Probably, the students are "turned off."

3. Indicates the teaching strategy being used.

Different teaching strategies call for different kinds of classroom interaction. Accordingly, we can work backwards to determine what strategy is being used by examining the classroom interaction. It may be, in some cases, that the strategy actually being used is not the one intended by the teacher. Or, it may be that the strategy being used, whether or not it is intended by the teacher, is inconsistent with the design of the curricular materials. (See Chapter 8 on Teaching Strategies for further details.)

4. Indicates in part the "hidden agenda" of the lesson.

Whenever we teach, we teach some things explicitly according to our plans. At the same time, we also teach some things implicitly or non-verbally. Some of these may be planned. Most of the time our non-verbal messages are not planned. Nor are we aware of them. For example, if a teacher consistently asks questions of the students and does little else while at the same time the students do little other than respond to the teacher, the teacher is communicating a non-verbal message. He is, in fact, saying to the student, "It is I in this classroom who asks the questions, and asking questions is my main role." In this way, the hidden agenda of a great amount of teacher question-asking may be to teach the students not to ask questions in the classroom. By examining the classroom interaction, we can infer in part some significant non-verbal messages communicated in the classroom.

AN EFFECTIVE, EASILY USED SYSTEM FOR OBSERVING PEDAGOGICAL INTERACTION

What follows is an observation system that we have successfully used in research and school supervision for observing classroom pedagogical interaction.

The Language of the Classroom System

    a. The Four Pedagogical Moves

    b. Examples of the Four Pedagogical Moves in Context

    c. Strategy for Using this System for Observing Pedagogical Interaction

    d. Example of Using the Language of the Classroom System

a. THE FOUR PEDAGOGICAL MOVES

Pedagogical Moves are verbal actions in teaching. There are 4 pedagogical moves, each defined according to the function it performs in the interaction.

1. *Structuring.* Structuring moves serve the pedagogical function of setting the context for subsequent behavior by either launching or halting-excluding interaction between students and teachers. For example, teachers frequently launch a class lesson with a structuring move in which they focus attention on the topic to be discussed during that session or the activity to be performed.

Examples of structuring moves:

    A. Let's turn to our topic of Cells and Food.

    B. Now, when President Kennedy saw that Cuba was creating a troubled situation, he called his advisors together. They decided that we should support an invasion of Cuba. Kennedy then. . . .

    C. We're going to stop here for today since this is a good breaking point in our discussion on *Richard III.*

In Example A, the speaker *structures* by *launching* a new topic. He *announces* the topic only—he does not speak on the topic, and he does not tell us anything substantive about Cells and Food, the topic he launches.

In Example B, on the other hand, the speaker *structures* by *launching* a topic dealing with President Kennedy and Cuba. Here, the speaker simply begins talking *on the topic*, whereas in Example A, the speaker talks *about* the topic. The speaker makes statements and, indeed, tells us something substantive about President Kennedy and Cuba.

In Example C, the speaker *structures* by *halting* the discussion of Shakespeare's play Richard III. The class knows that the discussion is over but it does not know yet what is coming next.

2. *Soliciting.* Moves in this category are designed to elicit a verbal response, to encourage persons addressed to attend to something, or to elicit a physical response. All questions are solicitations, as are commands, imperatives, and requests.

Examples of soliciting moves:

D. What is the chemical formula for water?

E. Please study the diagram on the chalkboard.

F. Jonathan, please turn off the lights so we can begin our film.

In Example D, the speaker solicits by requesting a verbal response about the formula for water. In Example E, the speaker solicits by requesting someone to mentally attend to the diagram on the chalkboard. In Example F, the speaker solicits by requesting Jonathan to perform a particular physical activity. In each case, we know what the expectation is simply by understanding the communication embodied in our language.

3. *Responding.* These moves bear a reciprocal relationship to soliciting moves and occur only in relation to them. Their pedagogical function is to fulfill the expectation of soliciting moves, thus answers to questions are classified as responding moves.

Examples of responding moves:

G. H_2O. (To the question, "What is the chemical formula for water?").

H. & I. No verbal responses to the 2nd and 3rd soliciting moves above since Examples E and F require non-verbal responses

J. Because I sprinkled the lawn. (To the solicitation, "why is the lawn chair wet?")

In Examples G and J, the speaker responds by answering soliciting moves, which required verbal responses. Responses to Examples E and F do not involve words; they require the giving of attention and the switching off of the lights. Hence, we cannot list responses in Examples H and I here but can only describe them.

4. *Reacting.* These moves are occasioned by a structuring move, soliciting move, responding move, or prior reacting move, but are not directly elicited by them. Pedagogically, these moves serve *to modify* (by clarifying, synthesizing, or expanding) and/or *to rate* (positively or negatively) what has been said previously. Reacting moves differ from responding moves. While a responding move is always *directly elicited* by a solicitation, reacting moves are *only occasioned* by preceding moves. Rating by a teacher of a student's responses, for example, is designated as a reacting move.

Examples of reacting moves:

K. I agree with your comment about President Kennedy and also think that he was correct in admitting his error publicly.

L. That's a good answer, Suzanne.

In Example K, the speaker reacts by first agreeing with a previous comment (see Example B) and then expanding on that comment. The agreeing part of the reaction is, in effect, a positive rating of that other pedagogical move.

In Example L, the speaker reacts by simply rating a preceding statement. The speaker gives a positive rating to the response by Suzanne.

Note that, in each example, the speaker did not directly have to make these statements. The speaker could have done something else. For example, after the statements made in Example B the next speaker could have asked a question, such as, "Did President Kennedy include Vice President Johnson in these meetings?" For this reason we say that Example K is a reacting move, since it was *occasioned* by another, preceding move. Example K is a reacting move and not a responding move since no other preceding move directly elicited it.

Example L is similar. The speaker did not have to rate Suzanne's response. The speaker could have asked another question or even opened up a whole new topic. The speaker chose to react and the response serves as only the occasion for the reaction.

These four pedagogical moves, *structuring*, *soliciting*, *responding*, and *reacting*, provide a means for describing what goes on in the classroom. These four names of the moves are technical names. So we must keep their definitions in mind and use the four words accordingly when discussing classroom interaction, lest we confuse the matter.

b. THREE SETS OF PEDAGOGICAL MOVES IN CONTEXT FOR FURTHER CLARIFICATION:

1. M. Structuring : Now, let's talk about the Grand Canyon.
   N. Soliciting : How was the Grand Canyon formed?
   O. Responding: It was formed by a river cutting through the rocks. (Response to Solicitation N)
   P. Reacting   : Very good, Ruth. (Reaction to Response O)

2. Q. Soliciting : Tell me where Jonathan's room is.
   R. Responding: Upstairs. (Response to Solicitation Q)
   S. Reacting   : No, downstairs and to the left. (Reaction to Response R)

3. T. Soliciting : And the President of the U.S.A., please?
   U. Reacting   : That question is too easy. (Reaction to Solicitation T)
   V. Reacting   : I don't think it's too easy. (Reaction to Reaction U)
   W. Response   : Richard Nixon, I believe. (Response to Solicitation T)

c. STEP BY STEP PROCEDURE FOR USING THE LANGUAGE OF THE CLASSROOM SYSTEM TO OBSERVE PEDAGOGICAL INTERACTION

(Before we begin here, let us be clear that this strategy is just for observing pedagogical interaction. Many supervisors will wish strategies for improving pedagogical interaction based on this procedure. They should see the Application section which appears later in this chapter.)

Step 1. Read carefully the definitions and examples of the four pedagogical moves so you are familiar with all of them.

Step 2. Schedule an observation period with the teacher. Plan for a visit of at least 15 minutes. Use a shorter period only if it constitutes an entire lesson.

Step 3. Observe the classroom. Use the Observing Pedagogical Interaction Form in Figure 5-1 to help you record your observations. Use it in this way:

a. Begin observing without taking any written notes. Keep in mind the four pedagogical moves and note only mentally the general pace of the interaction.

b. Make a mental note of the frequency of each of the four pedagogical moves.

c. Choose a short section of the interaction which you think will be fairly representative of what is going on. You will need at least a 2-minute sample.

d. Begin checking each move in the appropriate space on the form as it occurs. For each new move drop down one row. In this way there will be but one check for each row.

e. If the pace of the interaction is fast, you might need two blank forms for even a short sample.

f. Wait a while and choose another short sample to record on the Observing Pedagogical Interaction Form. (See Figures 5-2 and 5-3 on the next few pages for an example of a completed form.)

Step 4. Examine the completed forms from Step 3 as well as your mental notes asking yourself, "Who does what?"

a. Who performs the role of structuring?

b. Who solicits?

c. Who responds?

d. Who reacts?

e. What in general is the role of the teacher?

f. What in general is the role of the student?

(See Figures 5-2 and 5-3 for an example of Step 4) Note that a pattern begins with a Structuring or Soliciting move.

Step 5. Look for any patterns that seem to reappear during the interaction. Here is a list of the 6 most common patterns according to our research. There are indeed others but they occur infrequently:

1. Soliciting	2. Soliciting	3. Soliciting
Responding	Responding	Responding
Reacting		Reacting
		More Reacting

Person Observed _____ Observer _____

Date: _____ Time: _____

Observing Pedagogical Interaction (Speaker and Move)

	TEACHER				STUDENT			
	RESPOND	STRUCTURE	REACT	SOLICIT	RESPOND	REACT	SOLICIT	STRUCTURE
1								
2								
3								
4								
5								
6								
7								
8								
9								
10								
11								
12								
13								
14								
15								
16								
17								
18								
19								
20								
21								
22								
23								
24								
25								

Figure 5-1
Observing Pedagogical Interaction Form

Person Observed __Wayne Reese__ Observer __Jack Sommer__

Date: __10/2/__ Time: __10:03__

Observing Pedagogical Interaction (Speaker and Move)

	TEACHER				STUDENT			
	RESPOND	STRUCTURE	REACT	SOLICIT	RESPOND	REACT	SOLICIT	STRUCTURE
1								
2		✔		✔				
3					✔			
4			✔					
5				✔				
6					✔			
7			✔					
8				✔				
9					✔			
10				✔				
11					✔			
12				✔				
13					✔			
14			✔					
15				✔				
16					✔			
17			✔					
18		✔						
19				✔				
20					✔			
21							✔	
22	✔							
23				✔				
24					✔			
25			✔					

Figure 5-2

Observing Pedagogical Interaction Form—Completed (First Time Period)

Person Observed **Wayne Reese** Observer **Jack Sommer**
Date: **10/2/** Time: **10:18**

Observing Pedagogical Interaction (Speaker and Move)

	TEACHER				STUDENT			
	RESPOND	STRUCTURE	REACT	SOLICIT	RESPOND	REACT	SOLICIT	STRUCTURE
1				✔				
2					✔			
3				✔				
4					✔			
5				✔				
6					✔			
7			✔					
8				✔				
9					✔			
10						✔		
11			✔					
12				✔				
13					✔			
14					✔			
15					✔			
16				✔				
17					✔			
18			✔					
19				✔				
20					✔			
21					✔			
22			✔					
23				✔				
24					✔			
25					✔			

Figure 5-3

Observing Pedagogical Interaction Form—Completed (Second Time Period)

4. Soliciting	5. Soliciting	6. Structuring
Responding		Soliciting
Maybe some Reacting		Responding
More Responding		Reacting
More Reacting		

(See Figures 5-4 and 5-5 for examples of this Step 5)

Step 6. Write up some observations and comments about what is going on in the classroom pedagogically.

d. Example of using the Language of the Classroom System to observe Pedagogical Interaction

1. On the preceding pages are two completed "Observing Pedagogical Interaction Forms." The first form (Figure 5-2) was filled out during the first five minutes of class time after the class settled into its science lesson for the day. The second form (Figure 5-3) was filled out during the same lesson 15 minutes later. (per Step 3)

2. Who does what pedagogically in this classroom? (per Step 4 of step by step procedure for using the language of classroom system to assess pedagogical interaction. Shown in Figures 5-2 and 5-3.)

The teacher does the structuring. (2 times)
The teacher does the soliciting. (16 out of 17 times = 94%)
The student does the responding. (19 out of 20 times = 95%)
The teacher does the reacting. (9 out of 10 times = 90%)
In general, the role of the teacher is to solicit student responses and react to the responses.
In general, the role of the student is to respond to the teacher's solicitations.

3. Are there any patterns? (per Step 5 of the previously listed strategy. Yes, there appears to be two common patterns:

    a. Teacher Solicits—Student Responds
    b. Teacher Solicits—Student Responds—Teacher Reacts

There doesn't appear to be any particular order of these two patterns.
(See Figures 5-4 and 5-5 for examples of marked up completed forms as an aid to answering the two questions above.)

4. Comments (per Step 6 of strategy listed earlier)
The teacher seems to be the most active person by far. The teacher makes most of the pedagogical moves. The student is restricted essentially to responding to the teacher. The pace is a fairly fast one. The key element in the class is the questioning by the teacher. Usually there is but one answer to each question asked. Towards the end of the observation, as noted in Figure 5-5 the teacher began getting several responses to a question.
This classroom fits the general flavor of most classrooms according to research findings.

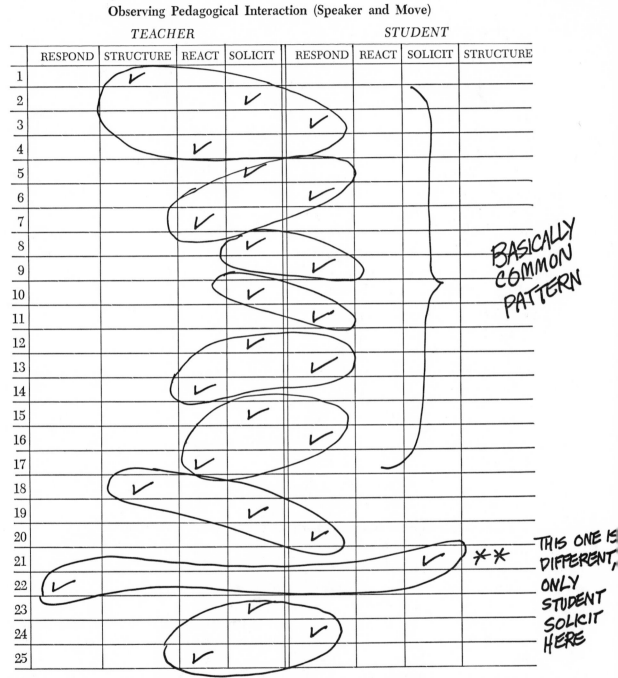

Figure 5-4
Observing Pedagogical Interaction Form—Completed—Showing
Both Basic Common Pattern and Student Solicit Pattern

64

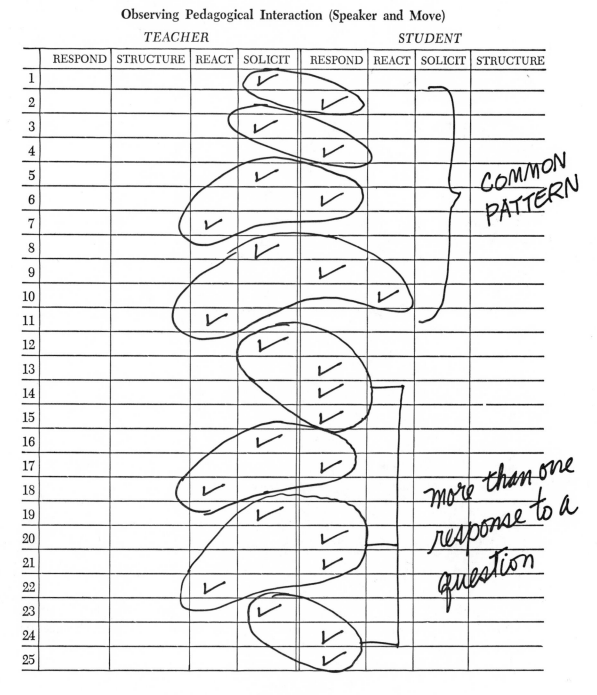

Figure 5-5
Observing Pedagogical Interaction Form—Completed—Showing
Both Common Pattern and Multi-Response Pattern

65

APPLICATION: HOW TO USE THE LANGUAGE OF THE CLASSROOM TO IMPROVE PEDAGOGICAL INTERACTION

It is one thing to observe a teacher's pedagogical interaction. It is another thing to help teachers improve the pedagogical interaction of their classrooms. The step by step strategy listed earlier is one for observing or describing interaction. Here, we shall turn our attention to several short strategies for helping teachers move toward more varied, balanced interaction. You may choose any one or more of these strategies to use with your teachers.

a. Several Short Improvement Strategies

Strategy A—whose feedback interaction is:

Supervisor's Description of Teacher $\longleftrightarrow$ Teacher's Self-Preference

Step 1

In Figure 5-6, which follows, you will find a composite sheet asking two main questions about pedagogical interaction. With the teacher, go over the four pedagogical moves, which are listed briefly on the top of the sheet as a reminder.

Step 2

Ask the teacher to answer Question I, "Who should make which move," with approximate percentages.

Step 3

Go over the examples of pedagogical patterns which are listed. Explain that these patterns are simply recurring sets of moves and that there are obviously many more possible ones. You can draw on the other listed patterns covered previously.

Step 4

The teacher, alone or with you, can list some other pedagogical patterns he can devise by combining pedagogical moves and speaker.

Step 5

Ask the teacher to answer Question II, "Which patterns should there be," with approximate percentages.

Step 6

Observe the teacher for at least 15 minutes. During the observation fill out the "Observing Pedagogical Interaction Form," as shown in Figure 5-1, which describes the teacher's classroom.

Step 7

At the end of the observation, add your comments about "who *did* what, and what patterns *occurred*." Use your completed forms here as a basis.

Name _____   Date _____

My Preference for _____

4 Pedagogical Moves

Structuring: launching or halting/excluding new topic; activity;
Soliciting: eliciting a verbal, physical, or mental response
Responding: fulfilling expectation of a soliciting move
Reacting: clarifying, expanding, synthesizing, or rating previous moves

Approximately

I   Who should make which moves?

Structuring: _____% Teacher   _____% Student
Soliciting: _____% Teacher   _____% Student
Responding: _____% Teacher   _____% Student
Reacting: _____% Teacher   _____% Student

II Which patterns should there be?   **For Example Only:**

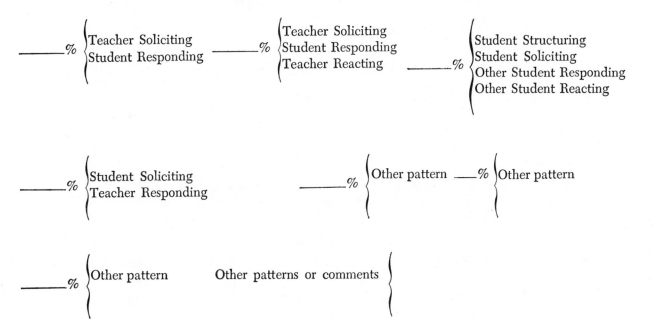

_____% { Teacher Soliciting / Student Responding }   _____% { Teacher Soliciting / Student Responding / Teacher Reacting }   _____% { Student Structuring / Student Soliciting / Other Student Responding / Other Student Reacting }

_____% { Student Soliciting / Teacher Responding }   _____% { Other pattern }   ___% { Other pattern }

_____% { Other pattern   Other patterns or comments {

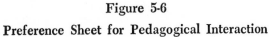

Figure 5-6

Preference Sheet for Pedagogical Interaction

67

Step 8

Give the teacher a copy of your description of his pedagogical interaction.

Step 9

If the teacher would like to discuss the description and his own preferences with you, by all means confer with him.

Step 10

In 2-4 weeks observe again, report your description again to the teacher, and confer with the teacher about the similarities and contrasts in the two observations.

Strategy B—whose feedback interaction is:

Supervisor's Description of Teacher ⟷ Teacher's Self-Description

Step 1

Schedule an observation visit with the teacher you are supervising.

Step 2

Observe the teacher for at least 15 minutes. During the observation fill out the "Observing Pedagogical Interaction Form," as shown in Figure 5-1, which describes the teacher's classroom.

Step 3

At the end of the observation, add your comments about "who *did* what, and what patterns *occurred*." Use your completed forms here as a basis.

Step 4

Ask the teacher to write out his answers to "who *did* what, and what patterns *occurred*."

Step 5

Confer with the teacher about the similarities and contrasts in the two descriptions—the class as it appeared to you and the class as it appeared to the teacher.

Strategy C—whose feedback interaction is:

Teachers B, C & D's Description of Teacher A ⟷ Teacher A's Self-Preference

Steps 1 to 5

These 5 steps are the same as the first 5 steps in Strategy A. Ask each teacher you supervise to fill out the *preference* form on pedagogical moves.

Step 6

Ask the teachers to organize themselves into trios or quartets for observation purposes.

Step 7

Ask each trio or quartet to prepare and submit an inter-teacher observation plan.

Step 8

Have teachers observe each other and share *descriptions of their colleagues* via the feedback from the "Observing Pedagogical Interaction" forms and comments.

Step 9

Ask each trio or quartet to report briefly in writing the results of their efforts.

Step 10

Confer with each trio or quartet to review their report.

Strategy D—whose feedback interaction is:

Students' Description of Teacher $\longleftrightarrow$ Teacher Self-Preference

Steps 1 to 5

These 5 steps are the same as the first 5 steps in Strategy A. Ask each teacher you supervise to fill out the *preference* form on pedagogical moves.

Step 6

Arrange with the teacher you supervise for some of his students to be observers.

Step 7

Explain the 4 pedagogical moves to the students. Ask them to observe and fill out the "Observing Pedagogical Interaction Form" (Figure 5-1). Ask them to add any comments.

Step 8

Ask the students to give their descriptions and comments to the teacher.

Step 9

If the teacher wishes, confer with him to discuss the similarities and contrasts between the students' descriptions and his own self-preference statement.

Strategy E—whose feedback interaction is:

Supervisor's Preference for Teacher $\longleftrightarrow$ Teacher's Self-Preference

Step 1

Fill out the preference form on pedagogical moves showing *your preferences* for the teacher you are supervising.

Steps 2 to 6

These 5 steps are the same as the first 5 steps in Strategy A. Ask the teacher you supervise to fill out the preference form on pedagogical moves.

Step 7

Confer with the teacher. Compare your preferences for the teacher with his self-preferences. Begin with points of agreement. Keep in mind that there is not a "right" viewpoint but only alternatives.

Figure 5-7 summarizes the 5 short strategies presented above.

b. SUMMARY OF FEEDBACK INTERACTIONS

Strategy A: Supervisor's Description of Teacher ⟷ Teacher's Self-Preference

Strategy B: Supervisor's Description of Teacher ⟷ Teacher's Self-Description

Strategy C: Teachers B, C, & D's Description of ⟷ Teacher A's Self-Preference
Teacher A

Strategy D: Student's Description of Teacher ⟷ Teacher's Self-Preference

Strategy E: Supervisor's Preference for Teacher ⟷ Teacher's Self-Preference

Figure 5-7
Summary of Feedback Interactions

c. What's the Idea Behind the 5 Improvement Strategies

Perhaps you have already noticed that there is an essential common feature to all these 5 improvement strategies. All of these strategies rely on the same factor as motivation for change—dissonance. Dissonance, for example, is the discrepancy between a person's perception or preference of his behavior and his actual behavior. Or, dissonance could stem from a person's preference about his behavior and someone else's preference about that behavior.

Now, according to Leon Festinger, the noted researcher on dissonance and author of the book *A Theory of Cognitive Dissonance*, dissonance is a motivating force for its own reduction. That is to say, when a person feels dissonant there is motivation for him to reduce the dissonance. Dissonance is a tension which people seek to reduce or remove once they are aware of it.

Strategy A creates a dissonance between the teacher's behavior (as described by the supervisor) and the teacher's preferred behavior. Strategy C and Strategy D create a similar dissonance between behavior and preference but these times the behavior is described by fellow teachers and students. Strategy B creates a dissonance between the teacher's behavior as described by the supervisor and the teacher's behavior as seen by himself. Strategy E creates a dissonance between the supervisors preference and the teacher's preference. In each strategy, the teacher becomes aware of the dissonance when in Step 8 or Step 5 he receives feedback from the supervisor, his fellow teachers, or his students.

These 5 strategies raise dissonance within the teacher simply because virtually all teachers are not now teaching the way they would like to and most teachers are now poor describers of their own behavior. Yet, there is no guarantee that all teachers will feel dissonant. There will be a few rare teachers whose behavior matches their self-preference, or self-description, or their supervisor's preference for them. For these few teachers these strategies will serve to maintain their rare condition rather than improve it.

Once the teacher feels dissonance, he will seek to remove or reduce it. There are several ways a teacher can do this. For example:

1. He can *reject or blur the incoming data.* By claiming that the data is too general, for example, a teacher can remove the dissonance.

2. He can *change his behavior.* In this way his behavior becomes consonant with his preferred behavior.

3. He can *change his preference.* In this way his preference becomes consonant with his actual behavior.

Our research shows that when teachers receive *specific feedback* they will change their behavior in order to reduce dissonance. Only when there is high dissonance, do teachers change their self-preferences.

In short, most teachers *will change their behavior* to bring it in line with their preference since they are not greatly dissonant. It may take some effort to change behavior but it is easier for most teachers to change their behavior than their preferences, which they have held for a long time as the foundation of their professional lives. And this change is desirable. Experience shows that when there is dissonance between classroom climate behavior and classroom climate preference, the preferred pedagogical interaction is the more positive climate. So, the *change in behavior is to a more positive pedagogical interaction.*

What is significant about these 5 improvement strategies is that the reliance on dissonance as the motivation for change eliminates the need for pressure from the supervisor. The teacher's own dissonance acts on the teacher. The supervisor does not have to "come down hard" on the teacher to bring about change. There is no need for lectures and urgings by you. Teachers already hold a more positive view on classroom climate than they are now implementing. For this reason, you can securely call upon other teachers, as well as students, to give feedback as a way of alerting the teacher to the dissonance between his preferred behavior and his actual behavior.

In one case, Strategy E, there is no observation of the teacher and, hence, no feedback is given about the teacher's actual behavior. Nevertheless, the effect of this strategy is positive, because the teacher is sensitized to pedagogical interaction in a concrete manner. No longer is pedagogical interaction an intangible, unexpressible idea.

What is more, the teacher now knows your beliefs about pedagogical interaction. He knows your preferences specifically. Since he is no longer in the dark about your preferences and hence expectations as a supervisor, the teacher can begin with you to meaningfully discuss pedagogical interaction in the school.

TAKING SOME FURTHER STEPS

Obviously, you will need often to go beyond just discussing, in general, the flow of pedagogical interaction. You will often talk with the teachers about *how* they can implement some of the desired changes. Some teachers will have ideas about what and how to change on their own. Yet others will seek your suggestions and desire a mutual determination of changes.

It is advisable to set out only a few suggestions at a time. These few suggestions should be quite specific. Teachers can deal with suggested changes if there are only several at a time. Most teachers can change, provided they are not overwhelmed by a score of ideas which are general in nature. Teachers can effect change by implementing a *few specific activities* designed for their particular need at a given time.

Figure 5-8 on the following page provides a simple way to limit and to specify changes. Note that the form directs attention to something of particular concern regarding pedagogical interaction. This keeps the teacher's attention focused. The teacher who is sensitive to pedagogical interaction will tend to change other aspects as well when he works on improving one specific area. The form calls for emphasis on positive activities to help the teacher move on to change.

At the same time, the form asks the teacher and you to list some specific practices to avoid and to maintain. Neither the positive nor the negative is sufficient by itself. A blank form (Figure 5-8) follows, and a completed form (Figure 5-9) follows it to serve as an example. Note that in Figure 5-9, the emphasis is on questioning which, according to the research on teaching, plays a significant, central role in teacher-student interaction in the classroom.

CONCLUDING REMARKS

Pedagogical interaction patterns are an important aspect of the classroom. They convey a message about the role of the teacher in the classroom. A supervisor can help sensitize teachers to pedagogical roles and patterns by using the Language of the Classroom System, as shown in the various forms and questions presented in this chapter. Teachers can change their patterns of interaction with help from specific activities designed to lead them to emphasize different, more varied behavior. With helpful feedback and fruitful suggestions, the supervisor can guide the teacher effectively.

Teacher _____ Date _____

Supervisor _____ Class _____

On Pedagogical Interaction

Of particular concern

In the future aim toward

Some new activities to do:

    A.
    B.
    C.
    D.

Some practices to maintain/increase:

    A.
    B.
    C.

Some practices to stop/reduce/avoid:

    A.
    B.
    C.

Date for Re-Assessment? _____

Who Will do Re-Assessment? _____

Who Will/Can Help Teacher Change? _____

Figure 5-8
**Pedagogical Interaction Evaluation Form Specifying Changes—
Blank Form**

73

Teacher __Wayne Reese__   Date __10/31__

Supervisor __Jack Sommer__   Class __Science__

On Pedagogical Interaction

Of particular concern _Questioning by teacher & students; so much teacher talk_

In the future aim toward _More student questioning – hope to lead toward less teacher questioning_

Some new activities to do:

A. _More small group experiments to allow for cross talk – see Teacher's Guide of text_
B. _Group presents experiments & findings. Then other groups ask 2-3 questions each_
C. _Play "20 Questions." Do silent demonstrations & students ask questions to find out why_
D. _Slow down pace of the class; wait several seconds before talking_

Some practices to maintain/increase:

A. _Supervision of individual lab work_
B. _Student demonstrations & reports_
C. _Periodic requests for clarification questions_

Some practices to stop/reduce/avoid:

A. _Teacher doing all the experiments_
B. _Whole group recitations_
C. _Doing old experiments where the answer is already known_

Date for Re-Assessment? __11/51__

Who Will do Re-Assessment? __Wayne Reese__

Who Will/Can Help Teacher Change? _Everybody in the science section_

Figure 5-9

**Pedagogical Interaction Evaluation Form Specifying Changes—
Completed Form**

Chapter 6

How to Observe and Improve Cognitive Processes

6

How To Observe and Improve
Cognitive Processes

INTRODUCTION AND OBJECTIVES

A central feature of all teaching is thinking. Teachers aim to teach their students to think—not only to behave in certain ways or to spout lists of recalled data. But, since there are obviously different modes of thinking, the teacher and supervisor need to be alert to them, to know what kinds of thinking the students are performing.

In this chapter, we shall treat the importance of cognitive processes, present a simple instrument for observing the cognitive processes performed in the classroom, and then suggest ways of balancing these processes.

At the conclusion of this chapter, the reader should be able to:

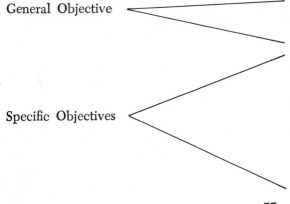

General Objective

1. Understand the significance and centrality of cognitive processes in teaching.

2. Describe three main types of cognitive processes used in teaching and some sub-types.

Specific Objectives

3. Use the verification instrument for observing cognitive processes.

4. Apply the verification instrument for balancing the cognitive processes in the classroom.

THE CENTRALITY OF COGNITIVE PROCESSES

Most people send their children to school to learn fundamental communication skills, computational skills, and thinking skills. People ask the teachers to concentrate not on, what to think, but on *how* to think. They want their children to be able, as the cliche goes, to think for themselves. This means that people value highly the cognitive aspect of school. They expect the teachers to emphasize cognitive processes and to plan for a variety of them so that students have a wide range of experience to draw on as they grow.

The emphasis on cognitive processes means that, as we look at teaching, we must note, not only the topic under study at a given time, but also the cognitive processes performed with that topic. For example, it is inadequate to simply observe that the teacher and students are dealing with the current events. We must look at what the teacher and students are saying about them. What cognitive processes are they performing? It is one thing to state facts; it is another to evaluate the deeds of the people involved. It would be possible for one teacher to spend a half an hour listing and briefly describing the key participants involved. On the other hand, it is equally possible for a second teacher to spend a half an hour analyzing the impact on the happening on the public and international diplomacy. Needless to say, the two classrooms of these teachers would be quite different even though both teachers are treating the same topic.

Since parents and educators are interested in teaching the students various cognitive processes, it is most important to note who is performing what in the classroom. We want to know who is doing the explaining or the evaluating. Is it the teacher or the student? For example, it is possible in a classroom for the students in a science experiment to gather much data related to combustion. Yet, it may turn out that it is the teacher who explains the cause and effect relationships and compares the present data to data from a previous experiment. In other words, the cognitive roles of the classroom in terms of what the teacher does and what the student does may be quite different. This difference may be significant if the students are generally restricted to performing a narrow range of cognitive processes. Furthermore, the students may also only be performing the simple task of stating facts whereas the teacher may be performing the more complicated and critical tasks of comparing facts and explaining facts. It is important, therefore, to know the distribution of cognitive roles in the classroom so that we can seek changes if necessary as we aim to provide students the opportunity to think for themselves.

These points about distribution and range of cognitive processes deserve further comment. It is most important, in our accelerated, 20th century technological life, that we learn fundamental skills and processes rather than a mere accumulation of data. Many of the facts that we know today will be obsolete, unnecessary, forgotten, or even obstructive in the future. People who have mastered a set of facts but not ways of dealing with those facts will find the future difficult. Those people who have had experience and success in a variety of ways of dealing with facts will find the future much easier to cope with. It is for this main reason that a student needs the opportunity to deal with a given topic under study in the classroom through a variety of cognitive processes. No topic and no subject field, in general, has a monopoly on a particular mode of thought or is restricted to a particular mode of thought. The field of English literature does not have a monopoly on evaluative interpretation just as physics does not have a monopoly on the presentation of specific facts.

It is clear from the above ideas on cognitive processes that teachers and students perform cognitive processes through words. People explain the cause of an event through language, by talking or writing. We give our opinions and support them primarily through words. (It is possible to give an opinion via a physical gesture such as a raised hand when we vote, or a raised eyebrow when we are skeptical about someone else's remarks. But the support for our opinions generally involves verbal language.) Thus, if we wish to observe and improve cognitive processes, we, then, must study the language of teaching. This is but another way to state that teaching is a linguistic activity. Language is the essential way that teachers and students state facts, offer explanations, and justify their opinions. It is through language that we perform cognitive processes.

In short, cognitive processes are at the heart of teaching. We establish a positive classroom climate (see Chapter 4) and strive for certain pedagogical interaction patterns (Chapter 5). We do so, in part, because we wish them to facilitate the performing of the essential task of teaching—thinking—as manifested in the cognitive processes we perform. We do this through language, which is the primary vehicle of communication between teacher and student.

AN EFFECTIVE, EASILY USED SYSTEM FOR OBSERVING COGNITIVE PROCESSES

What follows is an observation system that we have successfully used in research and school supervision for observing cognitive processes.

The Verification Method

a. The Three Main Types of Cognitive Processes

b. Comments on Specific Types

c. Strategy for Using the Verification Method to Assess

d. Example of Using the Verification Method

a. Three main types of cognitive processes

One way to view cognitive processes in teaching is to examine the statements and questions of the teacher and students. A *statement* is one kind of sentence. It is a sentence, which asserts that something is the case; it makes a truth claim; it manifests a cognitive process. (A statement may or may not be complete in terms of grammatical construction.) A *question* elicits a response from someone. We classify a question in terms of the type of statement it expects to elicit.

To examine statements and questions, we can use the *method of verification*, which means the way in which we discover if something is true. With the method of verification, we can classify statements and questions in teaching into three main types. In this way, we have three main types of cognitive processes.

1. *Definitional* (sometimes called *Analytic*)
Definitional statements are statements about the proposed use of language or other symbol system. These statements are necessarily true by virtue of the very words which compose them. For example:

   a. An import is a good coming into the country.

   b. Question: What does "we shall overcome" mean?
      Response: It means that, in the long run, we will win.

   c. Mi is the note that follows re in the scale.

   d. All of the trees in this group are called evergreens. Evergreen is just the label we give to these things.

   e. By "superstar" I mean, you know, like Wilt Chamberlain, Joe Namath, Billie Jean King, and Mark Spitz.

   To verify a definitional statement, we do not go for evidence to the world of our sense experience. We look rather to the various sets of rules about language or some other symbol system we have established. Note that Example C is necessarily true because mi is just another way of saying the note that comes after re.

2. *Empirical*
Empirical statements are statements which give information about the world based on our experience of it. To verify an empirical statement, we gather evidence via our sense experience. We observe the world and decide if the statement is true or false. For example:

   f. Spiro Agnew resigned as Vice-President.

   g. Every President has been a man.

   h. Most professional men tennis players earn more money than most women tennis players.

   i. If you put a cold bottle of water from the refrigerator onto the table, then it will sweat.

   j. Question: Why is the street wet?
      Response: Because the lawn sprinkler was at the edge of the grass.

   k. We import coffee from Brazil and Colombia.

   l. If President Kennedy had not been shot, we would have been out of Viet Nam much, much sooner.

3. *Valuative* (Sometimes called *Value* or *Evaluative*)
Value statements praise, blame, commend, criticize, or rate something. They deal with attitudes, feelings, morals, beliefs, and policies. To verify a valuative statement, it is necessary to know the criteria being used. For example, to verify the statement "Truman was a great president," it is necessary to know the criteria for being a *great* president. One person may be able to accurately

describe Truman's acts as a president and have a second person agree with him completely. But unless both persons share common criteria for what constitutes a great president, no amount of facts or accurate descriptions will provide a basis for determining the truth of the valuation statement about President Truman. If we do not know what the appropriate criteria are, then we cannot verify a valuative statement. For example:

m. *Hamlet* is better than *King Lear* or *Macbeth.*

n. I approve of our import policy so we can protect our own citizens from competition from the Orient.

o. Question: Do you believe we ought to have diplomatic relations with the government of mainland China?
Response: Yep, I think we should.

p. You can say what you want about their songs, but somehow, I still don't like the Beatles—they never did appeal to me. Yet, I really like the stuff Paul McCartney does on his own now 'cause he's more mature now and understandable.

b. comments on specific types

Obviously, within the three main types presented (definitional, empirical, and valuative), there are several specific types we can identify if we so choose. An easy way to treat these specific types is to examine the examples offered in the preceding section.

Under *Definitional* there is Example A, which gives a descriptive set of characteristics about the word "import" to tell us what it means. Example E does not do this. It simply gives some instances to which the word "superstar" refers. Yet, both Example A and Example C tell us what we mean by a particular word. Example B is like Example A but it refers to a phrase rather than a single word. Example D gives a label to a group of objects so we can have a name to call the group.

Under *Empirical* there are two principal types. (1) Examples F, G, and K all state facts. Examples F and K state *specific facts,* one past and one present, and Example G states a *general fact.* Nevertheless, the statements are all facts. (2) Examples H, I, J, and L all state some type of relationship among facts. In Example H, the statement compares/contrasts men and women tennis players. Example J states an explanation of the fact that the street is wet; it gives the cause (lawn sprinkler at the edge of the grass) for the effect (the street is wet). Examples I and L both are "If . . . , then . . ." statements also showing a relationship among facts. Even though we could never actually check at this point on the truth of a shorter war in Viet Nam because it is in the past, Example L is an empirical statement. It is contrary to fact now. So is the statement, "If we didn't have two arms, then we might just have one coming out from our chests." Such contrary to fact statements which are not verifiable are classified as empirical statements.

Under *Valuative* Examples, M and O simply express opinions; they do not offer reasons to support the opinions. In Examples N and P we have *opinions* and also *reasons to justify* these opinions.

From the above points, it is clear that, within the three main types of cognitive processes as determined by the method of verification, there are several specific types. In outline form, the cognitive processes look like this:

1. *Definitional*

   Definition of word or phrase giving set of applicable characteristics.
   Definition by giving instances to which the word applies.
   Label of a set of objects.

2. *Empirical*
   Facts
      Specific fact, past or present or even future.
      General fact, past or present or even future.
   Relationships and Purposes
      Compare/Contrast.
      Explain—show cause and effect.
      If . . . , then . . . . —present to future, verifiable in time.
      If . . . , then . . . . —contrary to fact, not verifiable.

3. *Valuative*
   Opinions
   Opinions with reasons to justify them.

One last important point here needs to be made. In any of these cognitive processes, it is one thing to offer statements in the course of a conversation as *new ones* in the discussion at hand. It is another thing to offer statements as *recalled* ones from a previous discussion or from a text, or film, or some other source. That is to say, it is one thing for a student to offer his own reasons, for example, about the continued popularity of Shakespeare. It is another thing for a second student to merely recall the reasons given by the textbook's author about the continued popularity of Shakespeare. In both cases, the statements giving reasons would be classified as empirical. Yet the first student is *thinking for himself productively*, while the second one is merely recalling someone else's thought.

c. Step by step procedure for using the Verification System to observe cognitive processes

(Before we begin here, let us be clear that this strategy is just for observing cognitive processes. Many supervisors will wish strategies for broadening the range and balancing cognitive processes based on this procedure. They should see the Application section of this chapter for such strategies.)

Step 1. Read carefully the definitions, examples, and comments on the three main types of cognitive processes so you are familiar with all of them.

Step 2. Schedule an observation period with the teacher. Plan for a visit of at least 15 minutes. Use a shorter period only if it constitutes an entire lesson.

Step 3. Observe the classroom. Use the Observing Cognitive Processes Form in Figure 6-1 to help you record your observations. Use it in this way:

Person Observed _____   Observer _____

Date: _____   Time: _____

Observing Cognitive Processes (Speaker and Type)

	TEACHER			STUDENT	
Valuative	Definitional	Empirical	Empirical	Definitional	Valuative
1					
2					
3					
4					
5					
6					
7					
8					
9					
10					
11					
12					
13					
14					
15					
16					
17					
18					
19					
20					
21					
22					
23					
24					
25					

✔ = occurred in simple form
✔ = occurred with relationships, reasons, or purposes given

Figure 6-1
Observing Cognitive Processes Form—Blank

a. Begin observing without taking any written notes. Keep in mind the three main types (and the specific types) if possible. Note, mentally, what is occurring in general, especially regarding the topic under study.

b. Make a mental note of the frequency of each of the three main types.

c. Choose a short section of the interaction which you think will be fairly representative of what is going on. You will need at least a 2-minute sample.

d. Begin checking each process in the appropriate space on the form as it occurs. You can check a cognitive process for each Teacher Pedagogical Move and each Student Pedagogical Move. (See Chapter 5 on Pedagogical Moves.) A simpler way is to concentrate only on Teacher Soliciting Moves, Student Responding Moves, and Student Reacting Moves. These moves, centering on the teacher questioning, are such a key element in teaching that they reflect the essence of what is going on cognitively.

e. If the speaker does more than one type in a single move, then check off more than one type per row. But, since more than one of the three types in a single move is uncommon, generally you will drop down one row for each cognitive type checked. In this way, there will generally be but one check in each row.

f. In order to get a more refined and informative picture of the classroom it is suggested that if the speaker asks for or gives relationships, or reasons, or purposes, then you should draw a line through your check. (See the bottom of the Observing Cognitive Processes Form and the sample completed forms in the next few pages.)

g. If the pace of the interaction is fast, you might need two blank forms for even a short sample.

h. Wait a while and choose another short sample to record on the Observing Cognitive Processes Form. Meanwhile take mental notes. (See Figures 6-1 and 6-2 for an example of a completed form.)

Step 4. Examine the completed form from Step 3 as well as your mental notes, asking yourself: "What is going on cognitively?"

Step 5. Write up some observations and comments about what is going on cognitively in the classroom.

d. Example of using the verification system to assess cognitive processes

Figure 6-2 is a completed "Observing Cognitive Processes Form." With it and some notes taken during the class period, it is possible to write the following comments.

Most of the class time devoted to the play *Hamlet* was spent in the empirical mode of thought. There were only a few instances of definitional and valuative

Person Observed _Joanne Romano_   Observer _B. Mayes_

Date: _12/10/_   Time: _1st Per._

Observing Cognitive Processes (Speaker and Type)

	TEACHER		STUDENT		
Valuative	Definitional	Empirical	Empirical	Definitional	Valuative
1		✔			
2			✔		
3	✔				
4				✔	
5	✔				
6				✔	
7		✔			
8			✔		
9		✔			
10			✔		
11			✔		
12		✔			
13			✔		
14		Ӈ			
15			Ӈ		
16		✔			
17			✔		
18			Ӈ		
19		✔			
20			✔		Ӈ
21			✔		
22	✔	✔			
23			✔		
24			✔		
25			Ӈ		

✔ = occurred in simple form

Ӈ = occurred with relationships, reasons, or purposes given

Figure 6-2

Observing Cognitive Processes Form—Completed

processes. Most of the time, the students followed the teacher's lead. This is so since the pedagogical pattern was one of teacher-question and student-response. When the teacher asked for a simple fact about the play, she got it. When she asked for reasons, she got them. In only one case did a student offer (empirical) reasons when not specifically asked to do so by the teacher (that is, Hamlet sent Ophelia to the nunnery to protect her). See Row 25 in Figure 6-2.

One student offered his personal opinion about Hamlet after stating that the setting of the play is medieval Denmark. He gave his opinion and supported it with reasons. ("I like Hamlet because I feel for him. He's not medieval, really, but modern. He sees conflict around him and doesn't know exactly what to do about it. That's how many modern people feel.") (See Row 20.) That was the high point not only of this short sample but also of the entire observation time of 25 minutes.

Most of the class time was empirical in that the teacher and students went over the events of the play. So this sheet pretty much reflects the entire observation time.

In general, the teacher set the type of cognitive process through her questions.

APPLICATION: HOW TO USE THE VERIFICATION METHOD TO IMPROVE COGNITIVE PROCESSES

It is one thing to observe the cognitive processes in teaching; it is another thing to help teachers improve their range and utilization of cognitive processes. The step by step strategy listed previously is one for assessing or describing cognitive processes. Here, we shall turn our attention to several short strategies for helping teachers move toward a varied, wider-ranged utilization of cognitive processes.

a. Several short improvement strategies

Strategy A—whose feedback interaction is:
Supervisor's Description of Teacher ⟷ Teacher's Self-Preference

Step 1

In Figure 6-3, you will find a preference sheet briefly describing the 3 main types of cognitive processes and asking two main questions. Go over the cognitive processes with the teacher.

Step 2

Ask the teacher to answer Question I with the appropriate percentages. Keep in mind the need for definitional may be relatively high for one topic while quite low for another. At this point there is no research known to the author which states optimum percentage for teaching.

Step 3

Ask the teacher to answer Question II either with a percentage or statement as to when reasons, comparisons, relationships, or purposes are appropriate, or some other comment about the use of the complex level within the three main types of cognitive processes.

Name _____   Date _____

My Preference for _____

Three Main Types * of Cognitive Processes Using the Verification Method

    1. Definitional—about the proposed use of language or other symbol system
    2. Empirical—give information about the world based on our sense experiences of it;
    3. Valuative—praise, blame, commend, criticize, rate something, or state a belief or policy

* For each type there can be reasons, relationships, causes, comparisons, or purposes given. Thus a *simple* type becomes *complex*. For example,

    EMPIRICAL SIMPLE: The road is slippery
    EMPIRICAL COMPLEX: The road is slippery because the truck spilled oil when it crashed.

I   In general I believe that in (my)(your) teaching there should be:

    _____% Definitional—Teacher
    _____% Definitional—Student   Questions and/or Statements
    _____% Empirical—Teacher   on Topic under Study
    _____% Empirical—Student
    _____% Valuative—Teacher
    _____% Valuative—Student

II   In general I believe that in (my)(your) teaching the *complex level* should be:

(fill in %, conditions when appropriate, or other comment)

Figure 6-3
Preference Sheet for Cognitive Processes

Step 4

Observe the teacher for at least 15 minutes. During the observation fill out the "Observing Cognitive Processes Form" (Figure 6-1) describing the teacher's classroom.

Step 5

At the end of the observation add your comments about what happened cognitively. Use your completed forms here as a basis.

Step 6

Give the teacher a copy of your description of the cognitive processes.

Step 7

If the teacher would like to discuss the description and his own preferences with you, by all means confer with him.

Step 8

In 2-4 weeks observe again, report your description to the teacher, and confer with the teacher about the similarities and contrasts in the two observations.

Strategy B—whose feedback interaction is:
   Supervisor's Description of Teacher ⟷ Teacher's Self-Description

Step 1

Schedule on observation visit with the teacher you are supervising.

Step 2

Observe the teacher for at least 15 minutes. During the observation fill out the "Observing Cognitive Processes Form" (Figure 6-1) describing the teacher's classroom.

Step 3

At the end of the observation add your comments about what happened cognitively. Use your completed forms here as a basis.

Step 4

Ask the teacher to write out his answers to "what happened cognitively."

Step 5

Confer with the teacher about the similarities and contrasts in the two descriptions —the class as it appeared to you and the class as it appeared to the teacher.

Strategy C—whose feedback interaction is:
Teachers B, C, & D's Description of Teacher A ⟷ Teacher A's Self-Preference.

Steps 1 to 3

These 3 steps are the same as the first 3 steps in Strategy A. Ask each teacher you supervise to fill out the *preference* form on cognitive processes.

Step 4

Ask the teachers to organize themselves into trios or quartets for observation purposes.

Step 5

Ask each trio or quartet to prepare and submit an inter-teacher observation plan.

Step 6

Have teachers observe each other and share descriptions of their colleagues via the feedback from the Observing Processes forms and comments.

Step 7

Ask each trio or quartet to report briefly in writing the results of their efforts.

Step 8

Confer with each trio or quartet to review their report.

Strategy D—whose feedback interaction is:
       Students' Description of Teacher $\longleftrightarrow$ Teacher Self-Preference

Steps 1 to 3

These 3 steps are the same as the first 3 steps in Strategy A. Ask each teacher you supervise to fill out the *preference* form on cognitive processes.

Step 4

Arrange with the teacher you supervise for some of his students to be observers.

Step 5

Explain the 3 main types of cognitive processes to the students. Ask them to observe and fill out the "Observing Cognitive Processes Form" (Figure 6-1). Ask them to add any comments.

Step 6

Ask the students to give their descriptions and comments to the teacher.

Step 7

If the teacher wishes, confer with him to discuss the similarities and contrasts between the students' *descriptions* and his own self-preference statement.

Strategy E—whose feedback interaction is:
Supervisor's Preference for Teacher ⟷ Teacher's Self-Preference

Step 1

Fill out the preference form on cognitive processes showing *your preferences* for the teacher you are supervising.

Step 2 to 4

These 3 steps are the same as the first 3 steps in Strategy A. Ask the teacher you supervise to fill out the preference form on cognitive processes.

Step 5

Confer with the teacher. Compare your preferences for the teacher with his self-preferences. Begin with points of agreement. Keep in mind that there is not a "right" viewpoint but only alternatives.

Figure 6-4 summarizes the 5 short strategies presented above.

b. SUMMARY OF FEEDBACK INTERACTIONS

Strategy A: Supervisor's Description of Teacher ⟷ Teacher's Self-Preference

Strategy B: Supervisor's Description of Teacher ⟷ Teacher's Self-Description

Strategy C: Teachers B, C, & D's Description of ⟷ Teacher A's Self-Preference
               Teacher A

Strategy D: Student's Description of Teacher ⟷ Teacher's Self-Preference

Strategy E: Supervisor's Preference for Teacher ⟷ Teacher's Self-Preference

Figure 6-4
Summary of Feedback Interactions

c. What's the Idea Behind the 5 Improvement Strategies

Perhaps you noticed already that there is an essential common feature to all these 5 improvement strategies. All of these strategies rely on the same factor as motivation for change—dissonance. Dissonance is the discrepancy between a person's perception or preference of his behavior and his actual behavior. Or, dissonance could stem from a person's preference about his behavior and someone else's preference about that behavior.

Now, according to Leon Festinger, the noted researcher on dissonance and author of the book *A Theory of Cognitive Dissonance,* dissonance is a motivating force for its own reduction. That is to say, when a person feels dissonant there is motivation for him to reduce the dissonance. Dissonance is a tension which people seek to reduce or remove once they are aware of it.

Strategy A creates a dissonance between the teacher's behavior (as described by the supervisor) and the teacher's preferred behavior. Strategy C and Strategy D create a similar dissonance between behavior and preference but these times the behavior is described by fellow teachers and students. Strategy B creates a dissonance between the teacher's behavior as described by the supervisor and the teacher's behavior as seen by himself. Strategy E creates a dissonance between the supervisors preference and the teacher's preference. In each strategy the teacher becomes aware of the dissonance when in Step 6 or Step 5 he receives feedback from the supervisor, his fellow teachers, or his students.

These 5 strategies raise dissonance within the teacher simply because virtually all teachers are not now teaching the way they would like to and most teachers are now poor describers of their own behavior. Yet, there is no guarantee that all teachers will feel dissonant. There will be a few rare teachers whose behavior matches their self-preference, or self-description, or their supervisor's preference for them. For these few teachers these strategies will serve to maintain their rare condition rather than improve it.

Once the teacher feels dissonance, he will seek to remove or reduce it. There are several ways a teacher can do this. For example:

1. He can *reject or blur the incoming data.* By claiming that the data is too general, for example, a teacher can remove the dissonance.

2. He can *change his behavior.* In this way his behavior becomes consonant with his preferred behavior.

3. He can *change his preference.* In this way his preference becomes consonant with his actual behavior.

Our research shows that when teachers receive *specific feedback* they will change their behavior in order to reduce dissonance. Only when there is high dissonance, do teachers change their self-preferences.

In short, most teachers *will change their behavior* to bring it in line with their preference since they are not greatly dissonant. It may take some effort to change behavior but it is easier for most teachers to change their behavior than their preferences which they have held for a long time as the foundation of their professional lives. And this change is desirable. Experience shows that when there is dissonance between classroom climate behavior and classroom climate preference, the preference for cognitive processes is the more positive climate. So, the *change in behavior is to a more positive cluster of cognitive processes.*

What is significant about these 5 improvement strategies is that the reliance on dissonance as the motivation for change eliminates the need for pressure for the supervisor. The teacher's own dissonance acts on the teacher. The supervisor does not have to "come down hard" on the teacher to bring about change. There is no need for lectures and urgings by you. Teachers already hold a more positive view on classroom climate than they are now implementing. For this reason you can securely call upon other teachers as well as students to give feedback as a way of alerting the teacher to the dissonance between his preferred behavior and his actual behavior.

In one case, Strategy E, there is no observation of the teacher and hence no feedback is given about the teacher's actual behavior. Nevertheless, the effect of this strategy is positive because the teacher is sensitized to cognitive processes in a concrete manner. No longer is cognitive processes an intangible, unexpressible idea.

What is more, the teacher now knows your beliefs about cognitive processes. He knows your preferences specifically. Since he is no longer in the dark about your preferences and hence expectations as a supervisor, the teacher can begin to discuss cognitive processes meaningfully with you.

TAKING SOME FURTHER STEPS

More so than with the other related observational frameworks you will often need to go beyond just discussing in general the flow of cognitive processes. You will often talk with your teachers about the appropriate balance among the three main types of cognitive as well as the appropriate utilization of reasons, comparisons, purposes, relationships and cause within the three types. You will often need to help teachers in implementing some of the desired changes. Some teachers will have ideas about what and how to change on their own. Yet others will seek your suggestions and desire a mutual determination of changes.

It is advisable to set out only a few suggestions at a time. These few suggestions should be quite specific. Teachers can deal with suggested changes if there are only several at a time. Most teachers can change, provided they are not overwhelmed by a score of ideas, which are general in nature. Teachers can effect change by implementing a few specific activities, which are designed for their particular need at a given time. To show this two case examples follow.

Case Example #1—High School

In an urban high school in New Jersey, the supervisor observed that the teacher and students were spending over 15% of their effort on definitional processes while, at the same time, spending about 1% with valuative. When he described this situation to the teacher, the decision was to alter these proportions, since both felt that they related closely to a lack of interest by the students in the books being read in this English course.

The teacher decided to open the next two lessons with the simple question, "Who is your favorite character and why?" The students' interest perked up especially when a secret written vote was taken for reading the book *1984*.

Case Example #2—Middle School (Grade 6)

During his first two visits to Harvey Thornton's sixth grade science class, the supervisor noted a significant amount of student questions, all of which asked for clarification. Some asked, "How come," others "Please explain that again," and others said, "I don't get it—say that again." In their feedback conference, Thornton and the supervisor felt that this high amount of questions probably stemmed from Thornton's procedure with laboratory demonstrations. Thornton would demonstrate an experiment silently, and then request one of his better students to *explain* what had happened. (For example, the student would explain why a bulb lights when you wire it to a

Teacher _____ Date _____

Supervisor _____ Class _____

On Cognitive Processes

Cognitive process or level of special concern _____

In the future aim toward _____

Some New Activities to Do:

    A.

    B.

    C.

    D.

Some Characteristics to Maintain/Increase:

    A.

    B.

    C.

Some Characteristics to Stop/Reduce/Avoid:

    A.

    B.

    C.

Date for Re-Assessment? _____

Who Will do Re-Assessment? _____

Who Will/Can Help Teacher Change? _____

Figure 6-5

Cognitive Processes Evaluation Form Specifying Changes—Blank Form

93

Teacher _J. Geary_   Date _12/5/_
Supervisor _B. Mayes_   Class _Soc. Studies_

On Cognitive Processes

Cognitive process or level of special concern _Valuative, with support for opinion spoken_

In the future aim toward _getting students to support their opinions but without threatening them_

Some New Activities to Do:

    A. _Role play a legislature proposing and passing bills, students need to convince others to vote their way_

    B. _In large group discussion, elect or appoint a "why person" who can request reasons when he feels group needs it._

    C.

    D.

Some Characteristics to Maintain/Increase:

    A. _Use of debates on policy issues in governmental topics_

    B. _Free exchange among students_

    C. _Frequent parental panelists to be interviewed / challenged_

Some Characteristics to Stop/Reduce/Avoid:

    A. _Students shooting off their mouths before prepared_

    B. _Teacher pushing for reasons when students are getting defensive_

    C.

Date for Re-Assessment? _1/15/_

Who Will do Re-Assessment? _B. Mayes_

Who Will/Can Help Teacher Change? _B. Mayes, H. Thornton, and Ted_

Figure 6-6

Cognitive Processes Evaluation Form Specifying Changes—Completed Form

battery.) Thornton assumed everyone understood what he did during the demonstration.

The supervisor and Thornton decided to add one more step to the demonstration procedure. Thornton, or one of his students, would carefully repeat the experiment twice. First, someone would *verbally* point out the steps which were taken and the results which happened. On the second time, someone else would give a running verbal account while a demonstrator silently repeated the demonstration. Thornton reported that the student clarification requests dropped because the basic data were now set before each student explicitly. Thornton had gone to the complex level of the empirical cognitive process too quickly.

Cognitive Processes Evaluation Form

Figure 6-5 provides a simple way to limit and specify changes. Note that the form directs attention to something of special concern regarding a cognitive process or level. This keeps the teacher's attention focused. The teacher who is alert to a cognitive process or level will tend to change other aspects as well when he works on improving one specific area. The form calls for emphasis on positive activities to help the teacher change.

At the same time, Figure 6-5 asks the teacher and you to list some specific characteristics to avoid and to maintain. Neither the positive nor the negative is sufficient by itself. A blank form follows (Figure 6-5) and a completed form (Figure 6-6) follows it to serve as an example. Note that in the completed form the special concern is on the support for opinions given, certainly a fundamental element in any social studies program.

CONCLUDING REMARKS

Cognitive processes are the essence of the teaching act. They are the thinking operations we do in the classroom. Through them we show what we consider significant about the topic under study. A supervisor can alert teachers to the main types of cognitive processes via the verification method. A supervisor can help a teacher achieve and/or maintain an appropriate balance among the three main types and between the simple and complex levels in each main type. Teachers can change if we help them with specific activities designed to lead them to a wide and balanced range of processes. With helpful feedback and fruitful suggestions, the supervisor can guide the teacher effectively.

Chapter 7

How to Observe and Improve Classroom Use
of Space and Student Groupings

97

How to Observe and Improve Classroom Use of Space and Student Groupings

INTRODUCTION AND OBJECTIVES

Within the past decade, there has been a decided effort by educators to change the schools. Teachers and supervisors have attempted to open up the school building and the classroom as well as the curriculum and their methods. The advocates of opening up the classroom by flexibly rearranging the physical dimension claim that many important results will ensue. Yes, significant results do occur when teachers open up their classroom, as shown in personal accounts and the research literature.

In this chapter, we shall treat the importance of the flexible use of space and student groupings, present a cluster of simple instruments for observing the use of space and student groupings, and then suggest some ways of helping teachers to be flexible in their use of space and groupings.

At the conclusion of this chapter, the reader should be able to:

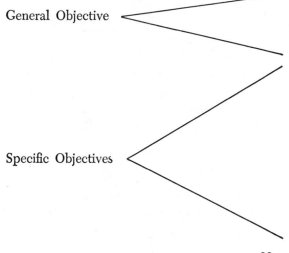

General Objective

1. Understand the importance and results of the silent message conveyed by the use of space and student groupings.

2. State some research results of flexibly rearranging the physical environment of the classroom.

3. Use the Rutgers Cluster of instruments for observing the utilization of space and student groupings.

Specific Objectives

4. Apply the Rutgers Cluster of instruments and model building to help teachers improve their utilization of space and student groupings.

THE FLEXIBLE USE OF SPACE AND STUDENT GROUPINGS

The current "in" term for describing informal education in the United States is "open education." This term serves as a focus for the re-direction of many classrooms toward an informal style. An essential element in open education is the flexible re-arrangement of the physical make-up of the classroom and the flexible grouping or students.

The idea of spacing and grouping is not a new one at all. Anthropologists such as Edward Hall, Raymond Birdwhistell, and Erving Goffman have for a long time investigated the relationship between space and communication. Their research shows that the distance people maintain between themselves is indicative of the type of communication they have. For example, with a distance of 8 to 10 feet and separated by a large desk, people have social and business communication which has a formal character about it. If people wish to be informal and have a personalized communication, then they must remain no more than four feet from each other. In this way, there is an interrelation between space and communication. That is to say, the distance in space influences, if not determines, the character of the communication. And, the character of the communication influences, if not determines, the distance people will maintain between them.

For some people, it is difficult to understand how the simple technique of rearranging the furniture and walls of a classroom can make a difference in teaching. Yet those educators who have tried this technique are convinced of the results. It is not only their personal experiences which bear this out. In a recent large-scale research project in northern New Jersey, supported by funds authorized under Title III of the Elementary and Secondary Education Act of 1965, the data show that "along with a physical change of the environment in Grades 1–3 has come a change in teacher behavior and a change in student attitudes. The nature of the rooms is such that interaction with large groups is virtually impossible. This has forced the teacher to interact with individuals and to organize classroom instruction so that individuals can react with one another. This has been coupled with, and hence presumably led to, an increase in children's perception of self worth and liking for school." (See the paper presented at the Annual Convention of the American Educational Research Association, February, 1973 by Tuckman, Cochran, and Travers.)

In the N.J. research project when the physical arrangement of the classroom encouraged and facilitated personal communication between the teacher and individual students or small groups of students rather than the whole class at one time, the teacher manifested more warmth and acceptance and the students felt more positive toward themselves. The interaction between spacing and quality of communication as well as well as the interaction between grouping and quality of communication is borne out by the evidence gathered in this research project. This is strong evidence which no serious, conscientious educator can dismiss.

Surely, not every educator will wish to make his classroom a prime example of open education. Nevertheless, the movement in education is toward more openness than previously achieved in the traditional classroom. The way a teacher arranges his classroom and the way he groups his students convey clear messages to the sophisticated observer. By his utilization of space and grouping of students, the teacher silently but clearly indicates what kind of teaching he wishes to and can perform. For this reason, supervisors will need to be able to observe, assess, and improve the use of space and grouping of students. The noted research anthropologist Edward T. Hall states in his classic book on social and personal space, *The Hidden Dimension,* "It is essential that we learn to read the silent communications as easily as the printed and spoken ones. Only by doing so, can we also reach other people, both inside and outside our national boundaries, as we are increasingly required to do."

A CLUSTER OF EFFECTIVE, EASILY USED INSTRUMENTS FOR OBSERVING THE UTILIZATION OF SPACE AND STUDENT GROUPINGS

What follows is a cluster of three instruments to help you, as a supervisor, observe the teacher's utilization of space and grouping of students. These instruments were developed at Rutgers University. Under my direction, and as part of his doctoral research, David Cochran developed these three instruments originally for use in a research program conducted by Professor Bruce Tuckman. The three instruments are all simple but highly effective.

The Rutgers Cluster

    a. Flexible Use of Space Scale (FUSS)

    b. Explanation and Directions for Using the Flexible Use of Space Scale

    c. Student Activity Measure (SAM)

    d. Explanation and Directions for Using the Student Activity Measure

    e. Grouping Measure (GM)

    f. Explanation and Directions for Using the Grouping Measure

    g. Examples of Using this Rutgers Cluster

a. Flexible Use of Space Scale (FUSS)

The purpose of the Flexible Use of Space Scale is to observe the conventionality of the utilization of space within the classroom. The instrument has two main parts—one devoted to the physical arrangement of furniture and walls and one devoted to the movement of people within the classroom.

The instrument appears in Figure 7-1. The Guide for the instrument follows in Figure 7-2. Following it are an explanation and the directions for using it. Look it over now.

b. Explanation and Directions for Using the Flexible Use of Space Scale

This FUSS instrument focuses on eight aspects of the classroom environment: (1) diffusion of desks; (2) use of floors for work areas; (3) decoration of walls and bulletin boards; (4) decoration of ceiling; (5) existence of display areas; (6) existence of partitions; (7) degree of student movement; and (8) degree of teacher movement.

Classroom Observed _____   Observer _____

Date _____ Time _____   Score _____

Flexible Use of Space Scale (FUSS)

I Physical Arrangement

A. Diffusion of Desks

| limited | moderate | extensive |

B. Use of floors for work areas

| limited | moderate | extensive |

C. Decoration of walls and bulletin boards

| limited | moderate | extensive |

D. Decoration of ceiling

| limited | moderate | extensive |

E. Existence of display areas

| limited | moderate | extensive |

F. Existence of partitions

| limited | moderate | extensive |

II Movement

G. Degree of student movement

| limited | moderate | extensive |

H. Degree of teacher movement

| limited | moderate | extensive |

Score: limited = 1;   moderate = 2;   extensive = 3

Figure 7-1

Flexible Use of Space Scale (FUSS)—Blank Form

Flexible Use of Space Scale

Aspect	Limited	Moderate	Extensive
I			
A. Desks	Desks in rows; formal arrangement designed for whole class instruction	Desks in groups or U shape; arrangement to facilitate some grouping	Desks spread out; no desks; arrangement to facilitate diversity of activity
B. Floors	No one working on floor; no signs that the students use the floor as work area	1-3 students working on the floor; some evidence of students being allowed to use the floor, e.g., rugs or mats	Several students using the floor; evidence of much use of floor, e.g., materials on the floor, many mats, rug areas in use
C. Walls & Bulletin Boards	Minimal decorations, empty boards, no use of walls for decoration	Bulletin boards filled; some use of walls as display areas	All bulletin boards filled; walls filled; great use of students' work on bulletin boards and walls
D. Ceiling	Nothing on ceiling for decoration	Some items hanging from ceiling as decoration, e.g., 1-3 mobiles	Many hanging objects; great use of students' work to decorate the ceiling
E. Display Areas	0-2 display areas; little use by the students; displays not to be used by students	2-4 display areas; some use by students for performing activities	Many display areas; areas used as interest or learning centers; displays intended for performing activities
F. Partitions	No partitions; partitions not used to separate learning centers	1-2 partitions; partitions used to separate learning centers	3 or more partitions; partitions used to separate learning centers
II			
G. Student Movement	Little student movement; most students working in seats or in group with teacher; move with permission only	Students move within limits; some out-of-seat activity; use of some areas other than desks for work	Free movement; students move to areas around room; much out-of-seat activity
H. Teacher Movement	Little teacher movement; teacher centered in front of room or with a group	Teacher moves to some extent; still maintains primary focus in one area	Teacher moves freely throughout the room; works with several individuals or groups

Figure 7-2

Guide for Flexible Use of Space Scale (FUSS)

The observer rates each aspect on a 3-point scale

●——●
limited   moderate   extensive

The extreme left position, called "limited," represents the most conventional instance of the aspect. The mid-point, called "moderate," represents a moderate deviation from conventional procedure. The extreme right position, called "extensive," represents a major deviation from conventional practice.

In order to make the scales specific for each aspect and to help the observer follow the guideline, examples appear in Figure 7-2.

You should become fully acclimated to the classroom before you begin to use this instrument. A wait of five minutes is usually enough. You then mark each aspect on instrument either limited, moderate, or extensive according to the guidelines given above. You must mark one point on the scale for each aspect.

To score the instrument use the following values:

        limited   = 1 point
        moderate = 2 points
        extensive = 3 points

The sum total for all 8 aspects will then be between 8 and 24 points. By assigning a numerical value you can compare classrooms with each other, or the same classroom with itself over time.

c. Student Activity Measure (SAM)

The purpose of the Student Activity Measure is to observe the number of different activities that are going on concurrently in the classroom. This instrument measures what the students are doing in the classroom in the various school subjects and their more specific topics.

The instrument appears in Figure 7-3. Following are an explanation and the directions for using it. Look it over now.

d. Explanation and Directions for Using the Student Activity Measure

This SAM instrument requires the observer to focus on at least four students. You may, if you so choose, use more students. When involved with many classrooms, we have used a sample of four students who are selected *at random*. You should use whatever range, from four students to the whole class, that works best for you.

Locate a student. Determine what subject he is involved in. You may ask him if you need to. If the subject is not clearly one of first seven listed but is a combination of two subjects (for example, a math/science activity such as measuring trees), then select the category "Broad Fields." If the subject is a single subject but it is not listed, then select the category "Other" and specify what that single subject is.

Next, determine which topic within the subject the student is engaged in. For

Classroom Observed ——————— Observer ———————
Date ——————— Time ——————— General Student Activity Score ———————
Number of Students Observed ——————— Activity Score ———————
Topic Score ———————
Subject Score ———————

Student Activity Measure

	MATH	LANG. ARTS	SOCIAL STUDIES	SCIENCE	ART	MUSIC	PHYS. ED. 1 HEALTH	BROAD FIELD	OTHER
Subject / Topic									
Listening to: Teacher									
: Peer									
Reading: Assigned									

Figure 7-3
Student Activity Measure (SAM)—Blank Form

Reading: Independ. Reference

: Independ. Pleasure

Writing: Program Instruction

: Workbook/Answ. Quest./Probs.

: Test

: Creative

Talk (Work Oriented) to: Teacher

: Peer

Talk (Social) to: Teacher

: Peer

Draw/Paint/Color

Construct/Experiment/Manipulate								
Utilize/Attend to A-V Equip								
Present play/panel/report: Group								
: Individually								
Recreate/Play/Take Break								
Disturb/Bother/Interrupt								
Wait/Day Dream/Meditate								
Distribute/Monitor/Class Routine								
Other (Specify)								

Figure 7-3 concluded

example, two students may both be involved in Math, but one may be engaged in the topic of adding while the other may be multiplying. Write in the topic pursued in a blank column under the appropriate subject.

Then proceed down the column until you find the row with the statement which describes the activity of the student (for example, Writing: Creative). Mark a tally in the cell which is the intersection of the appropriate row and column.

Do the same for each student you observe. You will have at least four tallies.

To score the instrument give one point for each cell marked. If your sample is four students, then you can score from one to four points only. That is, if all four students are engaged in the same activity with the same topic, then you will have four tallies in the same cell. The score will be one. If all four students are engaged in different activities and/or topics, then you will have tallies in four different cells. The score will be four. This is called the General Student Activity Score.

If you wish, you can also determine an activity score, a topic score, and a subject score. To do this, count the number of different rows, columns, or column groups that are marked. See Figures 7-7 and 7-8 for two completed forms.

e. Grouping Measure

The purpose of the Grouping Measure is to observe the extent to which students in a class function in various sized groups simultaneously. This instrument gives an indication of the flexibility of the grouping of the students at a given time.

The instrument appears in Figure 7-4. Following are an explanation and the directions for using it. Look it over now.

f. Explanation and Directions for Using the Group Measure

As you can readily see, the Grouping Measure resembles the Student Activity Measure. This Grouping Measure also requires you to focus on at least four students. You may use the same students here as you did before. This will simplify matters considerably if you do so. In any case, it is a good idea to use this instrument at the same time as the SAM instrument.

After you have randomly selected the students to observe, note the size of the group in which they are involved. Put a tally mark in the appropriate cell for each student you observe. That is, proceed down the column until you find the row with the statement which describes the activity of the student. Mark the cell which is the intersection of the activity and group size.

Do this for each student you observe. You will have at least four tallies.

To score the instrument give one point for each cell marked, just as with the SAM instrument. If your sample is four students, then you can score from one to four points only. That is, if all four students are engaged in the same Activity in the same group size, then you will have four tallies in the same cell. The score will be one. If all four students are engaged in different activities and/or group size, then you will have tallies in four different cells. The score will be four. This is called the General Grouping Measure Score.

Classroom Observed _____

Date _____ Time _____

Number of Students Observed _____

Observer _____

General Grouping Measure Score _____

Group Size Score _____

Activity Score _____

Grouping Measure

Group Size

	1	2	3-5	6-10	11-20	Whole Class
Listening to: Teacher						
: Peer						
Reading: Assigned						
: Independ. Reference						
: Independent Pleasure						
Writing: Program Instruction						

Figure 7-4
Grouping Measure—Blank Form

Writing: Workbook/Answ. Quest./probs.									
: Test									
: Creative									
Talk (Work Oriented) to: Teacher									
: Peer									
Talk (Social) to: Teacher									
: Peer									
Draw/Paint/Color									
Construct/Experiment/Manipulate									
Utilize/Attend to A-V Equip									

Present play/panel/report: Group						
Present play/panel/report: Individually						
Recreate/Play/Take Break						
Disturb/Bother/Interrupt						
Wait/Day Dream/Meditate						
Distribute/Monitor/Class Routine						
Other (Specify)						

Figure 7-4 concluded

Classroom Observed _J. Heater_   Observer _D. Cochran_

Date _2/26_ Time _10:30_   Score _22_

Flexible Use of Space Scale (FUSS)

I Physical Arrangement

A. Diffusion of Desks

limited	moderate	extensive ✗

B. Use of floors for work areas

limited	moderate ✗	extensive

C. Decoration of walls and bulletin boards

limited	moderate	extensive ✗

D. Decoration of ceiling

limited	moderate ✗	extensive

E. Existence of display areas

limited	moderate	extensive ✗

F. Existence of partitions

limited	moderate	extensive ✗

II Movement

G. Degree of student movement

limited	moderate	extensive ✗

H. Degree of teacher movement

limited	moderate	extensive ✗

   _0_   _4_   _18 = 22_

Score: limited = 1; moderate = 2; extensive = 3

Figure 7-5

Flexible Use of Space Scale (FUSS)—Completed Form—Showing High Score

Classroom Observed _L. Hartel_   Observer _D. Cohran_

Date __2/26__ Time __9:00__   Score _____

Flexible Use of Space Scale (FUSS)

I Physical Arrangement

A. Diffusion of Desks
| limited | moderate ✗ | extensive |

B. Use of floors for work areas
| limited ✗ | moderate | extensive |

C. Decoration of walls and bulletin boards
| limited | moderate ✗ | extensive |

D. Decoration of ceiling
| limited ✗ | moderate | extensive |

E. Existence of display areas
| limited | moderate ✗ | extensive |

F. Existence of partitions
| limited ✗ | moderate | extensive |

II Movement

G. Degree of student movement
| limited ✗ | moderate | extensive |

H. Degree of teacher movement
| limited ✗ | moderate | extensive |

4   8   0 = 12

Score: limited = 1;   moderate = 2;   extensive = 3

Figure 7-6

Flexible Use of Space Scale (FUSS)—Completed Form—Showing Low Score

Classroom Observed __J. Heater__   Observer __D. Cochran__

Date __2/26/__   Time __10:45__   General Student Activity Score __4__

Number of Students Observed __4__   Activity Score __3__

Topic Score __4__

Subject Score __2__

Student Activity Measure

Subject	MATH	LANG. ARTS	SOCIAL STUDIES	SCIENCE	ART	MUSIC	PHYS. ED. 1 HEALTH	BROAD FIELD	OTHER
Topic	Additions Balance / Tens + Ones				Airplane Model / Pictures + Slides				
Listening to: Teacher									
: Peer									
Reading: Assigned									
: Independ. Reference									

: Independ. Pleasure									
Writing: Program Instruction									
: Workbook/Answ. Quest./Probs.	X	X							
: Test									
: Creative									
Talk (Work Oriented) to: Teacher									
: Peer									
Talk (Social) to: Teacher									
: Peer									

Figure 7-7

Student Activity Measure—Completed Form—Showing High Score

Draw/Paint/Color	X								
Construct/Experiment/Manipulate		X							
Utilize/Attend to A-V Equip									
Present play/panel/report: Group									
: Individually									
Recreate/Play/Take Break									
Disturb/Bother/Interrupt									
Wait/Day Dream/Meditate									
Distribute/Monitor/Class Routine									
Other (Specify)									

116

Figure 7-7 concluded

Classroom Observed __L. Hartel__ Observer __D. Cochran__

Date __2/26/__ Time __9:15__ General Student Activity Score __1__

Number of Students Observed __4__ Activity Score __1__

Topic Score __1__

Subject Score __1__

Student Activity Measure

	MATH	LANG. ARTS	SOCIAL STUDIES	SCIENCE	ART	MUSIC	PHYS. ED. 1 HEALTH	BROAD FIELD	OTHER
Subject									
Topic	Addition								
Listening to: Teacher									
: Peer									
Reading: Assigned									

117

Figure 7-8

Student Activity Measure—Completed Form—Showing Low Score

: Independ. Reference									
Independ Pleasure									
Writing: Program Instruction									
: Workbook/Answ. Quest./Probs.	l l l l								
: Test									
: Creative									
Talk (Work Oriented) to: Teacher									
: Peer									
Talk (Social) to: Teacher									
: Peer									
Draw/Paint/Color									

Construct/Experiment/Manipulate							
Utilize/Attend to A-V Equip							
Present play/panel/report: Group							
: Individually							
Recreate/Play/Take Break							
Disturb/Bother/Interrupt							
Wait/Day Dream/Meditate							
Distribute/Monitor/Class Routine							
Other (Specify)							

Figure 7-8 concluded

If you wish, you can also determine an Activity Score and a Group Size Score. To do this, count the number of different rows (Activity Score) and different columns (Group Size Score) which are marked. See Figures 7-9 and 7-10 for two completed forms.

g. Examples of Using the Rutgers Cluster for Space and Grouping

Figures 7-2, 7-7, 7-8, 7-9 and 7-10 are completed examples of each of these 3 instruments. Please look them over now, for they show how to use this Rutgers Cluster of instruments on utilization of space and student groupings.

APPLICATION: HOW TO USE THE RUTGERS CLUSTER OF INSTRUMENTS TO IMPROVE THE UTILIZATION OF SPACE AND STUDENT GROUPINGS

It is one thing to observe spacing and grouping in teaching, it is another to help teachers improve their utilization of space and student groupings. So far, the procedures in this chapter have been for describing the use of space and groups. Here, we shall turn our attention to how to help teachers based on the data gathered with the three instruments.

The previous chapters on social climate, pedagogical interaction patterns, and cognitive processes each presented 5 short strategies for improvement. At this point, there is little need to present these strategies again. It will be quite easy for you to re-examine the 5 short strategies in any of these chapters and then apply them to this framework of spacing and grouping. For this reason, these strategies do not appear here.

Rather, we shall present a sixth idea, which is unique to this chapter. To help the teacher it will be most powerful and vivid to work together with a physical model of the classroom. There is no need here to present a lengthy justification of model manipulation and building. Creative and research literature is filled with successful examples of using models. Suffice it to cite the fantastic success with models which the biological research team investigating the DNA molecule had. See the account of their model building with Tinker Toy sticks and wheels in *The Double Helix* by James Watson, the scientist who won the Nobel Prize for his work in heredity with DNA.

For your model building you can use a simple "doll house" type model of the room and some doll house furniture. Or, you can use a cardboard model of the room with match stick furniture or cardboard furniture. The furniture and people can be realistically shaped or symbolically shaped. Choose your own shapes. It's fun. Whatever you choose you should be able to illustrate the classroom as you observed it and reported it with the three instruments. You may even ask the students in the classroom to construct the model for you. They will enjoy the project and benefit from it, too.

With the teacher first assemble the model to illustrate what the classroom now looks like. This will accustom you both to using the model. Then, begin to move pieces about, furniture and people, to conform to your preferences or experimental ideas. Or, with two models you can create a before and after pair for comparison purposes.

Classroom Observed __J. Hunter__

Date __2/26/__ Time __10:47__

Number of Students Observed __4__

Observer __D. Cochran__

General Grouping Measure Score __4__

Group Size Score __4__

Activity Score __3__

Grouping Measure

Group Size

	1	2	3-5	6-10	11-20	Whole Class
Listening to: Teacher						
: Peer						
Reading: Assigned						
: Independ. Reference						
: Independ. Pleasure						
Writing: Program Instruction						

121

Figure 7-9

Grouping Measure—Completed Form—Showing High Score

Category						
: Workbook/Answ. Quest./Probs.	/					
: Test						
: Creative						
Talk (Work Oriented) to: Teacher						
: Peer						
Talk (Social) to: Teacher					'	
: Peer						
Draw (Paint) Color				/		
Construct/Experiment/Manipulate			/			
Utilize/Attend to A-V Equip						

122

Present play/panel/report: Group						
Individually						
Recreate/Play/Take Break						
Disturb/Bother/Interrupt						
Wait/Day Dream/Meditate						
Distribute/Monitor/Class Routine						
Other (Specify)						

123

Figure 7-9 Concluded

Classroom Observed __L. Hartel__

Date __2/26__   Time __9:17__

Number of Students Observed __4__

Observer __D. Cochran__

General Grouping Measure Score __1__

Group Size Score __1__

Activity Score __1__

Grouping Measure

Group Size

	1	2	3-5	6-10	11-20	Whole Class
Listening to: Teacher						
: Peer						
Reading: Assigned						
: Independ. Reference						
: Independ. Pleasure						
Writing: Program Instruction						
: Workbook/Answ. Quest./Probs.						1 1 1 1

: Test

: Creative

Talk (Work Oriented) to: Teacher

: Peer

Talk (Social) to: Teacher

: Peer

Draw/Paint/Color

Construct/Experiment/Manipulate

Utilize/Attend to A-V Equip

Figure 7-10

Grouping Measure—Completed Form—Showing Low Score

Present play/panel/report: Group

: Individually

Recreate/Play/Take Break

Disturb/Bother/Interrupt

Wait/Day Dream/Meditate

Distribute/Monitor/Class Routine

Other (Specify)

126

Figure 7-10 concluded

You can create the classroom you prefer as you have indicated in the 5 short strategies applied from previous chapters.

As you re-design the classroom together, you can comment on the advantages and disadvantages of each new setting. Discuss the implications of the new designs. For example, the teacher may need to learn new techniques for teaching small groups of students. Try to create designs, which the teacher will be comfortable with and willing to change to in the real classroom.

Be flexible and create flexible designs. Keep in mind that flexibility in use of space and groups is a key element in opening up the classroom. Most educators recognize the desire and tendency of students to collaborate with their classmates when they are involved in exploring an interesting, exciting idea. Therefore, it is essential to create a classroom setting which facilitates the kind of education we prefer. The classroom setting should provide for various options by the teacher and students; it should accommodate frequent changes if needed; it should entice the student to learn; and it should provide many learning activities besides listening to the teacher. Research shows that even in the best classrooms, as judged by principals, only 50–60% of the students are actively engaged in attending or responding. In most classrooms, students are relatively inactive.

With positive designs and a positive atmosphere between you, the teacher can return to the actual classroom willing to improve the utilization of space and student grouping.

CONCLUDING REMARKS

The way a teacher uses space and student grouping conveys a silent, nonverbal message to everyone. Whether they are aware of it or not, the students receive this message, and the message has its definite effects on the teacher and students. You, as supervisor, can tune into this silent communication and give feedback about it to the teacher. With the Rutgers Cluster of instruments devoted to spacing and grouping, you can easily observe your teachers' classrooms. By using the 5 short strategies for improvement and the creating of designs with a model of a classroom you can help your teachers improve. Surely we must be alert to silent messages, just as we are to spoken ones.

Chapter 8

Teaching Strategies: What They Are
and How to Help Teachers with Them

Teaching Strategies: What They Are and How To Help Teachers With Them

INTRODUCTION AND OBJECTIVES

As we look at the educational scene today, we can easily conclude that there are several "in" terms which reflect areas of special interest. For example, in the area of nursery and primary intermediate and even secondary schooling the term *open education* serves as a focus for the redirection of many classrooms. Other "in" terms in education are *individualizing, behavioral objectives, accountability, teacher performance objectives,* and—*strategy.* Yes, the old, Greek-derived word, strategy, is an "in" word today.

This chapter, then, will examine the reasons for knowing about teaching strategies, the word *strategy* itself, the concept behind strategies, the rationale for two different strategies of teaching, and how to help teachers with strategy.

At the conclusion of this chapter, the reader should be able to:

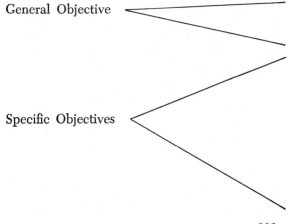

General Objective

1. Understand the nature of two different types of teaching strategies and how to help teachers with them.

2. State at least 3 reasons for knowing about strategy and how the concept of strategy applies to teaching.

Specific Objectives

3. State the ideas behind, advantages of, and disadvantages of the expository and discovery strategy types.

4. List some questions that can serve as the basis for helping teachers with teaching strategies.

REASONS FOR KNOWING ABOUT STRATEGY

The first reason for knowing about teaching strategies results from the attention given them by educators today. Strategies are "in" because educators realize that many recommended changes for our schools will simply not suffice. For example, closed circuit TV, open space facilities, and modular scheduling, separately or even together, will not necessarily alter the kind of interaction a teacher has with his students. These three changes, salutary as they are, do not deal with the essence of teaching but rather the facilitative aspects of teaching. Strategy deals with the essence of teaching, and for this reason, it is of central concern in these days of educational change.

There is obviously nothing more important that a supervisor can do than help his teachers constructively attain their goals. A sensitive and knowledgeable supervisor is constructive and enabling. If he can help teachers attain their goals through his own knowledge of teaching strategies, then the supervisor has fulfilled his mission. Since teaching strategies are at the heart of any teacher's attempt to achieve his goals, then the supervisor must know about them.

A teacher with a well-conceived and well laid out plan feels more comfortable, even if he leaves the plan while he teaches. A teacher can afford to leave his teaching plan temporarily because he has direction and security. Thus, a teacher's plan is most important to him, and the supervisor who know about strategies can help the teacher plan properly.

Another important task of the supervisor is the observance of his teachers, as pointed out in several chapters of this book. The supervisor who knows about teaching strategies will better be able to make sense of what he observes in the classroom. For example, suppose a supervisor observes the following pedagogical pattern (refer to Chapter 5): The teacher structures the lesson with an activity and then spends considerable time with the students collecting many specific facts through prodding questions. The knowledgeable supervisor, having identified the strategy, can understand what is going on as the teacher solicits multiple responses about the activity. He can relate the strategy to classroom climate, pedagogical interaction, and cognitive processes.

A supervisor's task often involves trouble-shooting. Some teachers get into trouble regarding their teaching effectiveness despite efforts to prevent it. The supervisor must work with teachers who often are teaching chaotically, and hence not achieving their goals. The supervisor who knows about teaching strategies can trouble-shoot, and with attention to an appropriate strategy, help the teacher out of his chaos.

Finally, the supervisor who knows about teaching strategies can teach them to his teachers. Not every teacher has studied, read, or formally learned about teaching strategies. The supervisor can help these teachers to learn about and subsequently implement appropriate teaching strategies in the classroom.

THE DERIVATION OF THE WORD "STRATEGY"

The word *strategy* derives from a military term. *Strategy* comes from the Greek word meaning *general*, which in turn is constructed of two roots meaning *to lead an army*. A general does not merely command his troops to attack the enemy. Rather, a general, or *strategos,* devises a plan whereby he considers the soldiers and material available, the space and the climate, the time, and his opposing forces. In short, the general devises a strategy to attain his goal and deploys his troops accordingly.

As our language developed, the concept of strategy has come to be used in other situations where the attainment of one's goal is blocked by someone or something. Thus, strategy is also employed in such games as chess, tennis, and basketball, in which one person or team matches ability with another person or team with the intention of overcoming competition. Strategy is used in other situations, too, where there is conflict, e.g., political race for office, world diplomacy, labor-management relations, and race relations.

THE CONCEPT OF STRATEGY APPLIED TO TEACHING

As always, we must ask whether the concept of strategy and its accompanying concepts of attack, retreat, force, enemy or opponent, and timing can be meaningfully applied to teaching. Are there sufficient similarities with war and chess, for example, to warrant the use of the concept of strategy in teaching? I would strongly argue that there are, that strategy applies closely to teaching. It applies because there are specified goals to be attained and obstacles to overcome in the classroom, and a variety of means can be used to do so.

Strategy applies to teaching just as it applies to any situation where goals are to be attained. That is, strategy in teaching is a plan for achieving the goal of learning, but that goal in no way implies a victory for the teacher and a defeat for the student. The teacher and student are to be viewed as cooperating in a plan that benefits both of them, but primarily the student. In the sense that a teaching strategy is a plan to attain certain goals and to guard against undesirable results, the concept of strategy is meaningful for teaching.

Strategy applies to teaching just as it applies to any situation where opponents or obstacles are to be overcome. The student is not the opponent of the teacher because the teacher and student are viewed as being in cooperation to achieve their goal. Indeed, in teaching there is no opponent to defeat but only obstacles to overcome. For example, a limited amount of time, and an inadequate reservoir of materials are obstacles to overcome. Other such items are out-of-school social pressures, prevailing peer attitudes, lack of previous preparation by the student for the given situation at hand, and a negative physical setting. In the sense that a teaching strategy is a plan to overcome the obstacles facing the teacher and the student, the concept of strategy is meaningful for teaching.

In applying the concept of strategy to teaching, we must focus on the goal to be attained rather than on the obstacles which must be overcome. Our attention must be on the goal, which is the basic determiner of our strategy. We shall return later to this application of the term strategy to teaching for further comment.

With these points about strategy in mind, we can offer the following *working definition* for "strategy," since many people prefer and need an explicit one:

Strategy is a carefully prepared plan
involving a sequence of steps designed to achieve
a given goal

THE RATIONALE FOR TWO CURRENT TYPES OF TEACHING STRATEGIES

The rise in interest in teaching strategies came during the past decade when educators sought new ways to revitalize the teaching process. Educators were aware that there existed more than one way to teach, but only one way predominated across the country. With the design of new curricular projects from nursery school through graduate and professional school came the need for a variety of teaching approaches, so as to have harmony among the various aspects of the innovative ideas. That is to say, the conception of certain projects called for a particular teaching approach. The curriculum could not be implemented (and, in fact, was not) unless teachers adopted a different way of teaching.

a. Expository Strategy

The present predominant strategy type in our schools may be called either *didactic teaching,* or *information-presentation teaching,* or *expository teaching.* The lecture and recitation are examples of this type of strategy. In this strategy: (1) The teacher sets forth the information to be received and learned by the student. The teacher here can be a live person or a substitute in the form of a textbook, film, recording, or computerized program. (2) The student receives and processes the information so as to understand the message transmitted. At times, the student seeks to understand a general idea or belief, and at other times to understand a range of specifics, depending on the message imparted by the teacher. (3) The student, then, particularizes or generalizes the message, perhaps through the aid of some check-up questions by the teacher, but mainly through his own cognitive efforts. (4) The student then applies this overall new message to his own life and then (5) acts upon it in situations related to it in the future.

This expository mode is based on the idea: (1) that the teacher knows what information the student needs to know, (2) that the teacher can effectively transmit his message to the student, (3) that the student can deal with the highly symbolic nature of this mode since the message virtually always comes through a verbal language, and (4) that the student can particularize or generalize, apply the message to his own life, and act on a symbolically derived message.

The teacher in this strategy becomes the more active participant physically and cognitively. He selects the knowledge, organizes it, tells it and re-tells it, making an effort to be clear and comprehensible, and questions the students to be sure that the student is learning. The teacher is the selector, organizer, imparter, synthesizer, questioner, and examiner. The student is a receiver. His cognitive task or load is not nearly as great as the teacher's.

The single greatest advantage of this expository mode is its efficiency. Via this strategy each generation can benefit from its predecessors. Were it not for our ability to learn through symbolic crystallization and transmission of cultural ideas, each generation would be forced, so to speak, to rediscover how to make fire, how to make a wheel, and how to write.

The disadvantages of this strategy are equally obvious. (1) Many people do not have the cognitive ability to cope with the symbolic qualities of this mode. (2) Therefore, their ability and opportunity to understand, and then apply the message, is limited. Indeed, these students may learn very little. (3) Furthermore, since the information or idea or belief comes from the teacher, the student may not even be interested enough to exert the necessary effort required in perceiving (note that *perceiving* requires more cognitive strain than *receiving*) and comprehending and applying the message. (4) The student may not exert the cognitive energy to particularize, generalize, or apply unless "forced" to by the teacher via threats, extrinsic rewards, or tests, all of which have their own well-known limitations.

b. Enabling Strategy

A second strategy type which is not as commonly used in our schools may be called *heuristic teaching*, or *discovery teaching*, or *enabling teaching*. Simulation games, brainstorming, sociodrama, and inquiry "lab" activities are examples of this type of strategy. In this strategy of teaching: (1) The teacher and students engage in some activity that presents a problem or conflict. The teacher and/or the students select the activity. (2) The teacher and students recount the essential elements of the activity so as to understand the particulars. (3) The student generalizes from the particulars some abstract principle or idea on his own, or through the guiding requests of the teacher, he generalizes, solves problems, or resolves conflicts. (4) The student, with the guidance of the teacher, if needed, applies the generalization to his own life through parallel situations. The student relates the activity and the generalization to analogous situations so as to have a connection between this activity and other aspects of his life. (5) The student acts upon the generalization in situations related to it in the future.

The enabling strategy is based on the idea: (1) that a person learns skills and knowledge and beliefs meaningfully when they stem from activity in which he participates; (2) that a person probably will act on generalizations when those generalizations arise from his own activity and his own generalizing; (3) that the student probably will see relationships among ideas and activities when he is physically and cognitively involved; (4) that the student need not translate all learning into a symbolic form in order for him to act on the learning; (5) that the teacher can at most guide, facilitate, enable, challenge, and prod the student to learn; and (6) that there is intrinsic motivation to learn—and remember—when there is a relevant problem to solve or a conflict to resolve.

The teacher in this strategy is not necessarily as physically active as the student. The teacher may participate with the student in the activity, but it is not necessary. It may indeed be advisable for the teacher to participate so as to establish a good working relationship with the student, to be aware of the particulars of the activity from which the student will generalize, and to maintain himself as an inquiring, learning person who understands the situation of a student seeking to solve a problem. The teacher is cognitively active as elicitor of the essential particulars of the activity, as guide to the interpretation of data, and as facilitator for gaining meaning from particular instances. The student is cognitively active as analyzer of the particular instances and as generalizer. He is obviously also physically active as the main person seeking the solution to the problem presented in the activity.

The advantages of this enabling mode are several. Students are more willing to learn when they have an active, relevant stake in the teaching situation. The student learns to "think for himself" as he solves a problem or resolves a conflict which motivates him. There is intrinsic reward for the student to participate and learn, stemming from the satisfaction received from solving a problem pertinent to him.

The disadvantages of this strategy are also several. (1) Because this strategy relies on meaningful activity, and because it is not possible to know in advance what will be all the particulars of an activity which pose a problem to the student, it is difficult to plan for teaching in great detail. (2) Not all people have the ability to generalize significantly from their own particulars. That is, not everyone can generate ideas, which are abstract enough so that they can then apply them meaningfully to related situations in the future. (3) In the short run, at least, this strategy is time-consuming, since it requires the generating of many particulars so as to create a solid foundation upon which to formulate some generalizations. (4) Because it is time-consuming and difficult to plan for, it is difficult in most teaching situations to "cover" a given area of study systematically and exhaustively. (5) Since the main aim in this mode is the creative, critical thinking required in solving the problem and then generalizing from the particulars of the activity, it is most difficult for the teacher to test the learning of the students.

HOW TO HELP TEACHERS WITH TEACHING STRATEGIES

From these descriptions of the expository strategy of teaching and the enabling strategy of teaching, it is apparent that neither one is, can be, or should be the only one a teacher uses with his students. What is more, whether we utilize expository teaching or enabling teaching, we should be alert to each's underlying ideas, advantages, and disadvantages. If not, we may not structure our behavior in a way which is likely to lead us to success with that strategy. For example, if I am teaching in the enabling mode but do not provide adequate time for generalizing and do not help students interpret their "raw" activity themselves, then my behavior is dissonant with the rationale for this strategy. And dissonance leads to trouble in teaching, unless it is removed.

Moreover, teachers not only must be consonant with the chosen strategy but must also be knowledgeable. We must keep underlying ideas and basic characteristics in mind as we match students, curriculum, and teaching strategy together. Though we may not be able to plan in great detail in the enabling strategy, we still can plan the "big" steps. That is, though we will not know every particular arising within an activity, we can project some essential ones, plan some key questions to facilitate generalization, and provide for adequate time. Though we may not be able to ensure that the message to be transmitted in the expository mode will be 100 per cent clear, we can plan for educational props to aid in reducing the strain of a high degree of symbolism and plan for feedback sessions, which emphasize the application of the message to the student's own life.

In both strategies, teachers will probably need to learn new teaching techniques if they wish to become more effective in attaining their goals. They will need to learn new questioning techniques so as to expand the student's ability to generalize, particularize, and apply the message. They will need to learn how to better enable, facilitate, guide, and challenge in the discovery mode. They will need to learn how to better communicate clear messages, organize, synthesize, and test in the expository mode.

It is clear from our experience with teaching that most teachers will need to concentrate on learning new techniques connected mainly with the enabling strategy. This is so because, in general, they have had precious little experience with the enabling strategy both as students and as teachers. Most people teach the way they were taught. As students they learned from their teachers a non-verbalized lesson on how to teach. They learned how to teach by participating with their teachers—in the expository teaching strategy.

When we look at the new curricular designs, we see a strong urging to utilize more and more discovery teaching opportunities. This is evidenced by the fantastic growth of simulation exercises and real, live experiences. Simulations and work-study programs constitute the basic activities, Step 1, in the enabling strategy. There is no dearth today of discovery opportunities for those who are alert to this strategy of teaching. Teachers who are alert will be able to utilize the activities that students have, both in and out of the classroom, towards a balanced teaching program.

The supervisor can help his teachers specifically by using the following sample questions as a checklist. The answers to such questions will provide helpful data in considering how strategy is used:

1. What roles does the teacher play while he is teaching—guide, enabler, facilitator, information-giver, tester, organizer? (See the role descriptions given in an earlier section of this chapter.)

2. What roles do the students play—receiver, analyzer, generalizer? (See the role discriptions given in an earlier section of this chapter.)

3. What tasks does the teacher perform? What tasks do the students perform?

4. Who asks the questions in the classroom? Who responds? If the students are asking the key questions, then probably the strategy is discovery.

5. What is the pattern of verbal interaction between teacher and students? (See Chapter 5.)

6. Who does the explaining in the classroom—giving reasons, purposes, relationships? That is, who performs the complex cognitive processes? (See Chapter 6.) If it is the teacher, then probably the strategy is expository.

7. What is the classroom climate, especially in regard to the dimension labeled Organized Demeanor? (See Chapter 4.) If the score for Organized Demeanor is quite high, then probably the strategy is expository, since this strategy requires strong teacher domination.

8. Does the physical layout of the classroom facilitate the flow of the steps in the strategy? (See Chapter 7.)

9. Are the students comfortable with the strategy being used? That is, is there a good match among student, content, and strategy?

10. Is the teacher learning new techniques to help him improve his implementation of the strategy?

11. What are the steps that comprise the teacher's plan to achieve the teaching goal? Do they follow each other sensibly?

The point of these questions is to alert the teacher to the desirability and necessity for consonance between his strategic intentions and his subsequent classroom actions. Obviously, the greater the consonance, the more likely that the teacher is aware of his strategy and able to implement his intentions.

The key roles of the supervisor are to:

(1) Help the teacher achieve *consistency within the steps* or tasks he performs so that the whole thing holds together neatly. This he can do by asking questions and planning the steps with the teacher himself.

(2) Help the teacher achieve *consonance between his intentions and his actions.* This he can do by observing the teacher teaching, and giving feedback so as to make the teacher aware of what is going on. This is important since research indicates that most teachers are not explicitly aware of their teaching acts. Many times teachers do not have carefully prepared plans. They often have only implicit, gut-level, partial plans. The chapters on observing, Chapters 4, 5, 6, and 7, offer the supervisor the instruments and procedures for gathering helpful data for this role.

ILLUSTRATIVE EXAMPLES OF STRATEGY FROM LESSON SCRIPTS

Below are two selections from lessons to illustrate the points concerning the identification of the two different types of strategy. Though the script of each is short, it is sufficient to get a flavor of the strategy being employed.

Read each selection carefully, keeping in mind the rationale for the strategies and the questions set forth earlier as aids in identifying strategy in teaching. Note the amount and type of teacher talk as key elements in the selection.

a. Expository Strategy

Teacher: We're sort of used to electric power today, aren't we? Do you notice I have some statements on the blackboard? These are magazine articles. Take a look at them for a minute: "Machines: Master or Servant?" "Slave Unaware." Does this give the idea that there might be some people today who are afraid of the machine? What's been happening in the railroad strike?

Student: A lot of people have been laid off.

Teacher: Because of machines, they have been laid off. And some airplane pilots, too. And some engineers. So, today there is even a fear of machines growing up. Well, how did we get started in this great use of machines? What is the era called?

Student: The industrial revolution.

Teacher: Good, the industrial revolution, a time when people had a striking change in their lives. There was a shift from hand work at home to machine work in the what?

Student: Factory.

Teacher: Factory, right. People started making things with machines outside of their homes, such machines as the spinning jenny and the water frame. This started in England and spread to its colonies later on. Because of the industrial revolution people developed the what? What industry did they develop?

Student: The coal industry.

Teacher: Right, they started mining coal for power to run the machines. Coal became very popular . . .

b. Enabling Strategy

Teacher: Boys and girls, yesterday's lesson dealt with the different kinds of people and jobs we find in a big, modern city like New York, London, or Buenos Aires.

Student: Someone said that London was a better place to live in than New York. Is that true?

Teacher: That's a very interesting question, Pat. To answer that let's start by looking again at these cities we've been studying now for the last week or so. What things can we identify about these cities?

Student: We heard people in that film speaking Spanish in Buenos Aires.

Student: They speak Spanish in New York, too. My grandmother lives there.

Student: But they speak mostly English in New York and London.

Teacher: How shall I list these facts on the board?

Student: In a chart, you know, with the three cities.

Student: I went to London once.

Teacher: What did you see there?

Student: Big Ben, London Bridge, and the Queen's guards—and we watched them change guards, too. That was neat.

Student: Did you see the Queen?

Student: No, but I—oh, I also saw some big square, I forgot the name now.

Student: I went to New York and saw lots of bridges and tunnels and even rode in the subway . . .

Teacher: Well, before you go, please copy down the chart I've been making on the board while you've been talking. See if there's any clue in it to help you answer Pat's question about which is a better place to live in.

Although we do not have a detailed statement of teacher objectives, or an explicit predetermined outline, or a pre-planned step by step sequence for us to inspect, it is surely possible from these two short selections to note several salient characteristics of each. We need to be able to do this since quite often a supervisor finds himself in a similar situation in the back of a classroom with only a note pad and his five senses to guide him.

In the first example, expository strategy, it is clear that the teacher sees himself as the main source of knowledge. He imparts facts and explanations. The students listen and sometimes answer what appears to be an "at-the-last-moment, fill-in-the-blank" question. In the second example, enabling strategy, the teacher picks up from a student question and leads the students to seek an answer via their own knowledge. The teacher's role is guide and enabler. The students contribute facts which are to become the basis for formulating an appropriate answer to the opening question.

If we had the lesson plans of these two teachers for these lessons, it would be possible to see the intended strategies clearly. Then, with a discussion with the teacher, we could (1) assess the match between curriculum, students, and strategy, as well as (2) determine the consonance between the intended and actual behavior. Here, however, we can only point out what the strategy is as seen through the actual interaction between teacher and student.

Sometimes it is not clear what strategy type is being employed. This is so because in practice many times strategies are not pure and distinct. Nevertheless, it is helpful to be able to identify and understand parts of the lesson.

A FURTHER LOOK AT THE METAPHOR OF STRATEGY

Before closing this chapter, let us return to the question of applying the term *strategy* to teaching in light of the above points.

I have asserted that it is appropriate to speak of strategy in teaching. Nevertheless, whenever we apply a term from one field to another, in this case from the military to education, it behooves us to be aware of possible dangers. The teacher is a leader but not a strategos or a general. The teacher's power of commanding his students to act in a certain way is severely limited. He cannot command a student to learn. The teacher who assumes the role of strict strategist, who expects a neat set of obedient responses, may indeed be creating a state of dependency in the student. And dependency is counter to the objective of independence, which is central in teaching.

The teacher who seeks to be a strategist, as well as the supervisor who is helping him, would do well to recognize the complexity of teaching and the complexity of learning, and should be willing to settle for an imperfect situation. The teacher and supervisor would do well to remember that students are students seeking to learn, rather than soldiers seeking to win a war. They surely must not fall into the trap of thinking that strategy is a plan to win a battle against the students, or the enemies. Woe to the teacher and the supervisor who consider students as enemies or opponents, or as cannon fodder to achieve their own personal goals. A teacher's strategy must be his overall, careful plan involving sequential steps and even alternative steps, so as to help the students and himself overcome any obstacles in achieving their goal.

Once the teacher is aware of the military metaphor of the term *strategy,* and notes the dangers of adhering too closely to this metaphor, he will not be confused. A teacher who is confused about his role by accepting and believing his metaphors goes on uncritically and behaves in accord with the concepts of his new images. Obviously, behavior befitting a "general at war" is undesirable in the classroom. And the supervisor's job is to help the teacher with strategy.

Chapter 9

How to Give Helpful Feedback

9

How to Give Helpful Feedback

INTRODUCTION AND OBJECTIVES

By now, it is obvious that the supervisor must go beyond observing in the classroom. Indeed, observing is but the first step in helping teachers. You, as supervisor, must report your observations to the teacher. Though it may seem perfectly clear to you what you observed, and though you may imagine that the teachers feel likewise, it is necessary to explicitly report back to the teacher. This is so because research shows that teachers are not able to accurately observe their classrooms while they are teaching. Hence, much of what you "feedback" to the teacher will be enlightening and helpful, especially if you employ some specific techniques.

In this chapter, we shall treat the importance of feedback in supervision, the characteristics and examples of helpful feedback, a scale for describing feedback, and some suggestions for practicing and giving feedback to teachers.

At the conclusion of this chapter, the reader should be able to:

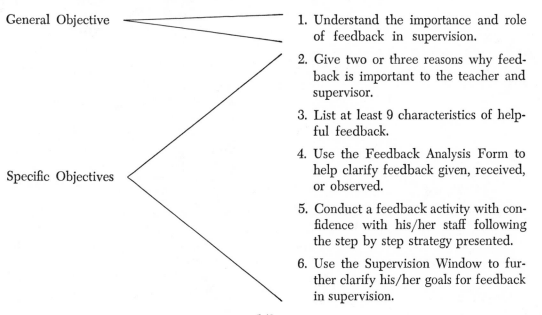

General Objective

1. Understand the importance and role of feedback in supervision.

Specific Objectives

2. Give two or three reasons why feedback is important to the teacher and supervisor.

3. List at least 9 characteristics of helpful feedback.

4. Use the Feedback Analysis Form to help clarify feedback given, received, or observed.

5. Conduct a feedback activity with confidence with his/her staff following the step by step strategy presented.

6. Use the Supervision Window to further clarify his/her goals for feedback in supervision.

The Importance of Feedback

Question: Who needs feedback?
Answer : Everyone!

If everyone needs feedback, then it must be important. And it *is* important.

Feedback is a relatively new word in our English language. Feedback means to use part of our output to go back into the input so as to keep the system within certain bounds. The classical example of feedback in our homes is the thermostat. By sending part of the heat from the furnace back into the thermostat to turn the furnace on or off we can control the heat produced by the furnace. Without feedback into the thermostat, the furnace would never know how well it is heating the room.

For example, *without feedback* the system looks like the one shown in Figure 9-1.

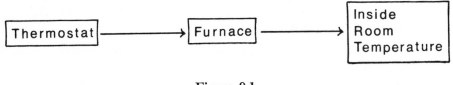

Figure 9-1

With feedback, the system looks like this:

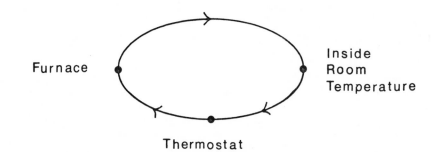

Figure 9-2

That is, with feedback which shows how warm the room is the thermostat will turn the furnace on or off.

Similarly, we can apply this concept of feedback *to human interaction.* The supervisor can serve as a "thermostat," the feedback element, to let the teacher know how his behavior is affecting other people. *Indeed, the purpose of feedback is to alert the teacher to the nature of his behavior, the effects of that behavior, and the perception you, as a supervisor, have of it.* Surely, the teacher gets feedback when he reads the students' faces, hears their comments, and sees their work. However, much of the time such feedback is indirect, unfocused, and self-selected. You, as supervisor, can give feedback to the teacher in a form which is organized and direct. You can give feedback on aspects of teaching which the teacher may not even be aware of on his own, and thus would never otherwise learn about them.

This idea of feedback for the teacher looks like this in diagram form:

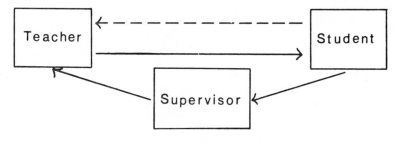

Figure 9-3

Note that there is some feedback from the student to the teacher, as mentioned earlier. But explicit, focused, and direct feedback comes to the teacher from the supervisor as he assesses the teacher's and students' performances.

Feedback to the teacher about what he is actually doing is most important. Most teachers are not performing the way they would like to. Moreover, most teachers are not fully aware of how their performances are affecting other people. They have but a vague, incomplete picture of their performance. Feedback on their performance is needed so that teachers can adjust their actions to match the needs of the situation, their own expectations, and the expectations of students, supervisors, peers, and parents.

Without feedback, the teacher has no way of *knowing* what effect his performance has. He may guess, imagine, or assume, but he doesn't know. Because he doesn't know, he cannot properly adjust his actions. A good example of this is the television teacher who tapes his lesson in an empty studio. Such a teacher must talk to other teachers and students who view the program, or else he will not get feedback for future lessons. Without feedback about actual performance, rather than expected or projected performance, the teacher cannot match future performances with the needs of the situation.

GIVING HELPFUL FEEDBACK

Since feedback will probably mean to the teacher that he will need to change his actions in some way, the teacher is likely to feel threatened. For this reason, you must be sure to take steps that will allow you to give helpful, meaningful feedback to the teacher. A teacher who is threatened may choose, deliberately or unconsciously, to disregard what you say. Or, he may even become so defensive as to lash out with attacks on you.

As supervisor, it is up to you to carefully organize and conduct the feedback session. You must take steps to create a positive atmosphere that will remove much of the threat the teacher feels. (It probably is impossible to remove all of the threat. There probably will always be some threat to the teacher whenever he meets with a supervisor, and you should keep this in mind.) Essential to this atmosphere will be your total efforts towards being trusted by your teachers. Here is the payoff for the many hours you spent and actions you took in establishing a trusting relationship between you and your teachers.

In addition, you will need to utilize all of your skills so that you can communicate effectively. Effective communication is extremely important and an entire, separate chapter on it appears following this one. The last two sections of that chapter, "Skills for Improving Communication" and "Further Suggestions on Effective Communication," are especially pertinent to giving helpful feedback. Rather than repeat the points made in those two sections, I shall request you to read the next chapter and consider the 5 skills and suggestions there as an integral part of this whole part of the book dealing with feedback and communication.

It is advisable to set up the physical environment of the conference room in a way which conveys a personal atmosphere. Arrange the chairs so that you can talk in soft tones and face each other without intervening barriers, such as a large desk to literally and figuratively keep you apart. On the other hand, you may need a small table on which to rest things. Perhaps the best arrangement is for you two to sit at right angles to each other at the corner of a table. This will permit close communication as well as a place to write and share written reports. This cross-corner arrangement is a better use of space for communication than a cross-talk or a side-by-side arrangement. (For more on the effect of the nonverbal use of space see Chapter 7 on How to Observe and Improve Classroom Use of Space and Student Groupings.)

At this point, it is appropriate to list some Characteristics of Helpful, Meaningful Feedback which will further aid you in giving feedback if you utilize them.

1. *Focus feedback on the actual performance of the teacher rather than on his personality.* Here, you should utilize your written and mental notes gathered during your observations. Use words which refer to the teacher's actions rather than his qualities as a person. For example, speak about "the fact that the pedagogical interaction pattern was teacher, question—student, response, for almost 20 minutes" (Chapter 5) rather than "the teacher is a controlling person in the classroom."

2. *Focus feedback on observations rather than assumptions, inferences, or explanations.* It is important to focus on what you heard or saw rather than on what you assumed went on or what you inferred was the meaning or explanation behind the performance. If you do make some interpretations based on your observations, then clearly identify them and ask the teacher to offer his own interpretations and comments. Preferably the observations you cite should be your own, rather than what someone else observed and passed on to you for transmission to the teacher. This focus will keep you on what you have observed rather than on motives, and thus the teacher will not be as defensive or threatened. For example, speak about "the fact that in each

visit to the classroom you observed all the children engaged in the same activity as a whole group" (Chapter 7) rather than "why the teacher is afraid to try small group teaching."

3. *Focus feedback on description rather than evaluation.* Since the purpose of feedback is to alert the teacher to what effect his performance is having, it is necessary to be descriptive rather than judgmental. In giving *feedback,* your task is to report on *what* is going on rather than on *how well* things are going. Description within a particular framework is non-evaluative. For example, speak about "the fact that the teacher asks simple questions on empirical data without reasons to support them" (Chapter 6) rather than "it is poor teaching to ask data gathering questions."

4. *Focus feedback on the specific and concrete rather than the general and abstract.* Feedback which is specific and concrete is helpful because the teacher can handle it himself. He can place the information in a time and place context and examine it there. He can make his own generalizations if he wishes. This situation is not nearly as threatening to the teacher as a generalization made by you, conveying the message of a trend over time, which may appear to be irreversible. For example, speak about "the teacher's score of 10 on the creativity dimension of the Tuckman Form" (Figures 4-2 to 4-7 in Chapter 4), rather than "the teacher always seems to be dull and pedestrian when December rolls around."

5. *Focus feedback on the present rather than the past.* Feedback, which is related to remembered teaching situations, is meaningful. If the teacher no longer remembers the events described in your observation, then he cannot use the feedback well. Your feedback should come soon after you observe and can report to the teacher. Then the teacher will still remember the events and be able to tie the feedback into a time and place context, thus enhancing the meaning of your remarks. Give feedback sooner rather than later, but also consider other variables such as the teacher's emotional state and yours, so that you time the feedback well.

6. *Focus feedback on sharing of information rather than on giving advice.* If you create an atmosphere of sharing, that you wish to offer what you have to the teacher for mutual consideration, then you create a non-threatening situation. If the feedback is *shared information,* then the teacher is free to use it as he sees fit in light of your overall conference comments. If you give *advice,* you are telling the teacher what to do. This sets up a threatening situation, since you show yourself to be better than he is by removing his freedom of action. For example, speak about "the teacher examining the data with you on the 15 questions he asked" (Chapters 5 and 6) rather than "I think you ought to ask more questions of those three cheerleaders sitting in the back of the room."

7. *Focus feedback on alternatives rather than "the" best path.* When you focus

on alternatives, you offer freedom of action to the teacher. You do not restrict him to your chosen path. The teacher is then free to choose from the alternatives explored which will best suit him and the situations he has in his classroom. He maintains his professional dignity and can accept the feedback without much threat. For example, speak about "increasing student participation by using small groups, and/or providing more activities, and/or using many mini-units so as to appeal to more students" rather than "the best way to get students to participate is to put them into small groups with their own leaders."

8. *Focus feedback on information and ideas phrased in terms of "more or less" rather than "either-or."* More or less terminology shows that there is a continuum along which the teacher's actions fall. Either-or terminology connotes an absolute situation of two extremes without any middle ground. More or less terminology is more appropriate to education where there are few, if any, situations with absolute positions. The many complex variables in teaching require us to keep a sliding continuum in mind without a predetermined extreme position. For example, speak about "asking less questions per lesson" rather than "either the teacher or the students should question but not both."

9. *Focus feedback on what the teacher, the receiver, needs rather than on what you, the sender, need to get off your chest.* Since the purpose of feedback is to alert the teacher about his performance, you must keep him in mind. Even though you may have several things on your mind which will impart a sense of release to you, your first consideration must be the meaningfulness of the feedback to the teacher. If you must get a few things off your chest, perhaps a separate conference or casual meeting would be better so as to differentiate the *feedback* session from your *release* session.

10. *Focus feedback on what the teacher can use and manage rather than on all the information you have gathered.* Though you have much data, you must resist the tempetation to overwhelm the teacher with your observations. The purpose of feedback will be destroyed if you overload the teacher and he feels helpless in the face of too much feedback. Keep the amount of feedback to a manageable level, the level which the teacher, not you, can handle.

11. *Focus feedback on modifiable items rather than on what the teacher cannot do anything about.* This point is obvious yet necessary and important. There is no value to the teacher in focusing on behavior which he cannot change. He will only feel that there is no hope. By focusing on what he can modify you offer him the opportunity to change and feel successful. This will create a positive atmosphere about feedback. For example, speak about "possible ways of rearranging the students' desks" rather than "the loud clicking of the clock disturbed some students."

12. *Focus feedback on what the teacher requests from you rather than on what you could impose upon him.* If at all possible, concentrate on the information

which the teacher requests from you. His request is a sign of interest and care. This information and any subsequent change in action can serve as a springboard into other meaningful aspects.

13. *Check the feedback you give by asking the teacher to summarize the points for both of you.* An excellent technique during a feedback session is to ask the teacher to summarize the main ideas raised between you. You will be able to check on what has been said. You will have a good way of gaining insight about the 12 suggestions listed above.

FEEDBACK ANALYSIS FORM

Based on the 13 characteristics of helpful, meaningful feedback presented in the previous section, it is possible to analyze a feedback session. The Feedback Analysis Form (Figure 9-4) used for this follows. It is one that we have found fruitful in analyzing a feedback session given, received, or observed. Look it over now.

Obviously, an excellent feedback session will be scored with all 1's because the more to the left the better. That is, the characteristics on the left describe a helpful feedback session. There is room in the right hand margin for writing some brief notes about the 13 items. You can use this form yourself and even give one to the teacher to use in analyzing what happened. You can also use it when you observe other supervisors at work.

When you read over a completed Feedback Analysis Form, you have a clear idea not only about what happened, but also about what you should strive to improve next time. The items and their markings offer you an easy way to set your goals for your next feedback session. A completed Feedback Analysis Form (Figure 9-5) follows to give an illustration of the usefulness of this form.

AN ACTIVITY FOR IMPROVING GIVING FEEDBACK

Just as it is important to improve other skills, it is also important to improve the giving of feedback. Most people need practice and help in implementing the characteristics of helpful, meaningful feedback into their supervisory sessions. To get such help, we have used the following technique. Note the many feedback opportunities in this activity as the roles change in the role playing trios. You can use this activity with teachers, other supervisors, or both together, since every faculty person can surely use help in giving feedback.

Step 1. Divide the group into trios. Try to have everyone in a trio. If there is one extra person, appoint him as Official Roaming Observer. If two people are extra, then join with them yourself to form another trio.

Step 2. Ask each trio to label its members A, B, and C.

Step 3. Read the following scenario:
"This is a feedback session between a supervisor and a teacher. The supervisor observed the teacher yesterday and noted many things. Chief among those in his mind is the fact that in using the Tuckman Form (Chapter 4) he scored the teacher 12 on Creativity and 41 on Orga-

Feedback Analysis Form

Giver _____ Date _____

Receiver _____

Observer _____

Below are 13 scales to use in analyzing the feedback you give or receive or observe. Analyze each item by circling the appropriate number on the scale.

Notes on particular instances

1. Emphasized performance   1 2 3 4 5 6   Emphasized personal qualities

2. Based on observations   1 2 3 4 5 6   Based on inferences

3. Descriptive   1 2 3 4 5 6   Evaluative

4. Specific & Concrete   1 2 3 4 5 6   General & Abstract

5. Well-timed   1 2 3 4 5 6   Poorly timed

6. Giver shared information   1 2 3 4 5 6   Giver gave advice

7. Emphasized alternatives   1 2 3 4 5 6   Emphasized "the" path

8. Framed in "more or less" terms 1 2 3 4 5 6   Framed in "either/or" terms

9. Based on receiver's needs   1 2 3 4 5 6   Based on giver's needs

10. Useful and manageable amount given   1 2 3 4 5 6   Overload given

11. Emphasized modifiable items   1 2 3 4 5 6   Emphasized non-modifiable items

12. Emphasized requested aspects   1 2 3 4 5 6   Emphasized imposed items

13. Checked receiver summarized   1 2 3 4 5 6   Unchecked receiver did not summarize

Figure 9-4
Feedback Analysis Form—Blank Form

150

Feedback Analysis Form

Giver _Leslie Walker_   Date _12/31_

Receiver _Donna Messer_

Observer _____

Below are 13 scales to use in analyzing the feedback you give or receive or observe. Analyze each item by circling the appropriate number on the scale.

			Notes on particular instances
1. Emphasized performance	1 ②3 4 5 6	Emphasized personal qualities	
2. Based on observations	1 ②3 4 5 6	Based on inferences	
3. Descriptive	1 2 ③4 5 6	Evaluative	
4. Specific & Concrete	1 2 ③4 5 6	General & Abstract	
5. Well-timed	①2 3 4 5 6	Poorly timed	*on next day*
6. Giver shared information	1 2 ③4 5 6	Giver gave advice	
7. Emphasized alternatives	1 2 3 ④5 6	Emphasized "the" path	*only one way given for rearranging the room*
8. Framed in "more or less" terms	1 2 ③4 5 6	Framed in "either/or" terms	
9. Based on receiver's needs	1 ②3 4 5 6	Based on giver's needs	
10. Useful and manageable amount given	1 ②3 4 5 6	Overload given	
11. Emphasized modifiable items	①2 3 4 5 6	Emphasized non-modifiable items	
12. Emphasized requested aspects	1 2 3 ④5 6	Emphasized imposed items	*added in stuff on climate anyhow*
13. Checked—receiver summarized	①2 3 4 5 6	Unchecked—receiver did not summarize	

Figure 9-5
Feedback Analysis Form—Completed Form

nized Demeanor (organization and control). The supervisor is concerned, and he is meeting with the teacher soon."

Step 4. Assign roles as follows for each trio.
Person A = Supervisor
Person B = Teacher
Person C = Observer

Step 5. Clarify roles. The Supervisor and the Teacher are to meet in conference. The Observer is to take mental and written notes. After the role play, the Observer will give feedback to the Supervisor and Teacher. He will paraphrase the session, beginning with the sentence, "As I understand it, here's what happened." (That is, the Observer will practice observing and giving feedback to his two partners.)

Step 6. Ask each trio to role play the situation. The Supervisor speaks first.

Step 7. After 3–7 minutes stop the role play, and ask the Observer to begin his paraphrase and open a short discussion in each trio.

Step 8. Ask the trio, separately or together, to fill out a Feedback Analysis Form (Figure 9-4) on the feedback of the Supervisor to the Teacher.

Step 9. The trio can now discuss the Feedback Analysis Form data as well as the comments of the Observer, Supervisor, and Teacher.

Step 10. After a short while begin a second role playing situation. Read the following scenario:
"This is a feedback session between a supervisor and a teacher. The supervisor observed the teacher and focused on teaching strategies. He believes he noticed a discovery lesson but several parts are fuzzy to him. He seeks clarification especially in the small amount of participation by two usually active students."

Step 11. Assign roles as follows for each trio:
Person A = Teacher
Person B = Observer
Person C = Supervisor

Steps 12-13-14-15. These are the same as Steps 6, 7, 8 and 9 above.

Step 16. After a short while begin the third and last role playing situation. Read the following scenario:
"This is a feedback session. The teacher has requested it. He is a bit unhappy. When the supervisor observed him, the teacher was not feeling up to par. He felt that things went wrong. The students were not as responsive as usual."

Step 17. Assign roles as follows for each trio:
Person A = Observer
Person B = Supervisor
Person C = Teacher

Steps 18-19-20-21. These are the same as Steps 6, 7, 8 and 9 above.

Step 22. After a short while, stop the trios' discussions. If you have an Official Roaming Observer, ask him to give a report now on what he heard and saw.

Step 23. *Debrief* the entire activity with the group. Allow adequate time since this debriefing is important and necessary.

   a. *Begin* the debriefing by encouraging the group to talk simply about what happened. This will review the activity and provide a foundation of data upon which to build in order to analyze, interpret, and learn from the activity.

   b. Focus the rest of the debriefing on such key questions as:

   Was it difficult to be the Observer? the Supervisor? the Teacher?

   When you heard the comments of the Observer, did you accept them?

   What kind of feedback from the Observer was helpful to you?

   What kind of feedback from the Supervisor was helpful to you?

   What further suggestions do you have for people giving feedback?

Step 24. Summarize, generalize, and conclude. Here is your opportunity to tie the whole activity together. Because in each of the three situations, both the Supervisor and the Observer give feedback and have the opportunity to practice giving helpful, meaningful feedback, you will have many points to utilize as raised in the discussion.

Step 25. Move forward. Use this activity to spring into another idea related to feedback. An excellent suggestion is the use of the Supervision Window which follows.

HOW TO USE THE SUPERVISION WINDOW

The Johari Window (Figure 9-6) is a device which allows us to look at ourselves in an illuminating way. The name derives from the two people, *Joe* Luft and *Harry* Ingham, who conceived the basic figure. The basic Johari Window, as you can see in Figure 9-6, is a 2x2 matrix developed around four key ideas, self, others, known, and unknown. Thus, there are four areas in the window.

   Area 1: This is the Public area—here are the things you know about yourself as well as what other people know about you.

   Area 2: This is the Blind or "Bad Breath" area—here are the things other people know about you but which you are not aware of yourself.

   Area 3: This is the Private area—here are the things other people do not know about you but which you do know about yourself.

Area 4: This is the Unknown area—here are the things other people do not know about you as well as the things you do not realize about yourself.

The Johari Window

	Known to Self	*Unknown to Self*
Known to Others	1 Public	2 Blind
Unknown to Others	3 Private	4 Unknown

Figure 9-6
The Johari Window

Within the window the four areas may grow or shrink as you learn more about yourself and as you disclose more about yourself to other people. There is no doubt that each of us learns more about himself every day, from our own activities and from feedback we receive. At the same time, we may not be revealing everything about ourselves to other people for whatever reason we choose.

With the basic idea in mind, we can draw Figure 9-7, which pictures how the Supervision Window might appear near the beginning of a supervision program you conduct with your teachers. Areas 2, 3, and 4 are bigger by far than Area 1. Area 4 is the biggest area, since the teacher does not have the benefit of observation and feedback yet. Area 3 is big simply because you have not yet observed much, and therefore you have not yet learned much about the teacher. Area 2 shows that you have done some observing already, but have not yet fed all the information you know back to the teacher. Your feedback is in appropriate amounts.

The Supervision Window

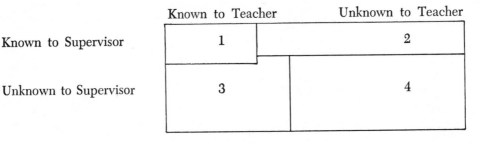

Near the Beginning of a Supervision Program
Figure 9-7

The interesting question now is: How do you think the Supervision Window should look after the supervision program you conduct has been in operation for some time? We have found it appropriate at this time to ask educators to draw their own Figure 9-8 before we reveal our own conception. So, in the space of the next sheet, draw your idea. Keep in mind that you can shrink or enlarge every one of the 4 areas. Try it now before moving ahead.

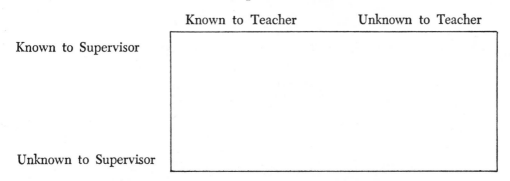

The Supervision Window

Known to Teacher   Unknown to Teacher

Known to Supervisor

Unknown to Supervisor

After Supervision Program Underway for Some Time

Draw your own idea of what the Supervision Window should look like.
Figure 9-8

When you draw your own idea of what the Supervision Window should look like, in effect you set your own goal for supervision. Indeed, things may not turn out the way you prefer them to, but you have an idea of how you would like them to look. For this reason, there is no single correct or incorrect drawing of Figure 9-8. My conception of what the Supervision Window should look like after some time appears in Figure 9-9.

Note that I have left something, however small, for each of the 4 areas. I mention this because I have seen drawings of other educators who have eliminated Area 4, Area 3, or Area 2. I prefer to keep some privacy in the figure. That is, I think it is healthy that there still be a Private area and an Unknown area. Also, I do not believe I can feed back everything I know to the teacher, and hence the Blind area must also remain. On the whole, I see the Public area growing largest and remaining the largest. Yet, as indicated by the arrows, each of the areas will shrink and expand as time changes.

You will find the Supervision Window an interesting springboard device to use with your faculty. Explain the basic idea to them as shown in Figure 9-6, and then present Figure 9-7 which shows the Supervision Window at the beginning of a supervision program. Then ask each person to draw his own Figure 9-8. Ask a few people to show their drawings so as to kickoff a lively discussion. Present your own Figure 9-8 to show your ideas about supervision. The exchange of ideas will be most interesting, especially if someone has some different ideas.

It is a good practice to discuss varying ideas of what supervision should be. If you and your faculty are working with different goals in mind and do not know it, then giving feedback will probably be trying and unsatisfying. If you find out about your differences early, then you have time to talk over your goals. With a better understanding of each other, you can conduct a more fruitful feedback program. The Supervision Window can help you in this part of supervision.

The Supervision Window

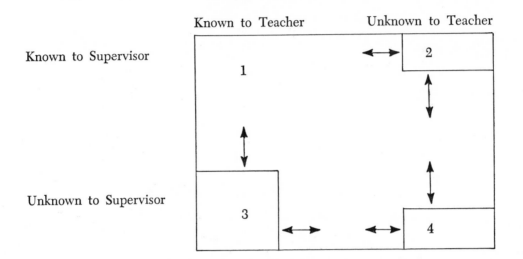

After Supervision Program Underway for Some Time
Figure 9-9

CONCLUDING REMARKS

Giving feedback to teachers is essential in supervision. Teachers, like everyone else, need feedback in order to adjust their actions in light of what they actually do rather than in light of what they expect or think they do. By following the characteristics of helpful, meaningful feedback listed earlier, and by employing skills which facilitate effective communication, you can create a sound supervisory session. You can practice giving feedback with teachers by participating in the feedback activity involving role-playing trios. You can follow up this activity by explaining and utilizing the Supervision Window in discussions with your faculty. All in all, practice and emphasis on feedback, as presented in this chapter, will help you in supervision.

Chapter 10

How to Communicate Effectively

10

How to Communicate Effectively

INTRODUCTION AND OBJECTIVES

Whether it deals with teaching students or supervising teachers, who would dare deny or even doubt the significance of good communication to the educational process? Neither I nor you, I'm sure. This is so because communication of ideas, feelings, and beliefs is a fundamental human necessity which underpins all our social interactions. Supervision is one such social interaction which particularly demands good communication, because the supervisor aims to help the teacher improve the teacher's communication with students.

In this chapter, we shall treat the centrality of communication to education, present an exercise to illustrate the effects of effective communication, and then suggest ways of applying these ideas with teachers.

At the conclusion of this chapter, the reader shall be able to:

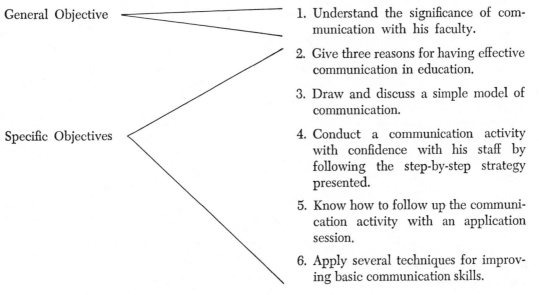

General Objective

1. Understand the significance of communication with his faculty.

2. Give three reasons for having effective communication in education.

3. Draw and discuss a simple model of communication.

Specific Objectives

4. Conduct a communication activity with confidence with his staff by following the step-by-step strategy presented.

5. Know how to follow up the communication activity with an application session.

6. Apply several techniques for improving basic communication skills.

EFFECTIVE COMMUNICATION

We need to communicate in order to live, to teach students, and to supervise teachers. We need *effective communication* if we wish to succeed in our tasks. Effective communication means that the receiver interprets the message he has received in the way the sender intended him to. If the receiver interprets the sender's message in a way not intended, then all kinds of negative consequences can occur. For example, let us suppose that you as a supervisor schedule a conference with a teacher. Your intention is simply to get some feedback so as to be aware of what is going on in the teacher's daily program. The teacher is tense and anxious because he feels that he is about to be evaluated. You open the conversation and ask, "Well, what's going on?" The teacher, already anxious, takes the question as a threat and a challenge. He answers with a sarcastic tone. The conference continues downhill and is a disaster, and each of you comes away with negative feelings.

Effective communication is the responsibility of the receiver as well as the sender, even though it is common to stress the sender's obligation to be clear. Communication is a two-way process. It is not possible for a sender to be clear—in the abstract. There is no such thing as one-person communication, that is, communication with a sender only. The sender must be clear to somebody—to a given receiver or group of receivers. The receiver, on the other hand, does not just receive messages. He receives messages from a given sender or group of senders. In short, communication, by its very nature, requires two persons. To have effective communication both persons, sender and receiver, must take steps. The sender must try to be clear to the receiver, keeping in mind his knowledge of the receiver's ability to communicate effectively with him. The receiver must try to listen to the sender, keeping in mind his ability to communicate effectively with him.

It is not simple or easy to achieve and maintain effective communication. Effective communication depends on mutual trust. Distrust reduces the accuracy of communication. Therefore, if you desire to communicate effectively with your teachers, then you, as a supervisor, must simultaneously work on establishing mutual trust in all your dealings with the teachers. Because of what has gone on in education for a long time, many teachers are indeed distrustful of supervisors. Mutual trust between supervisor and teacher requires constant alertness.

Connected with mutual trust are two other qualities central to effective communication—mutual confidence and mutual empathy. The person who is confident, or at least seeks to become confident, can communicate effectively. He does not distort messages that might otherwise threaten another, unconfident person. Similarly, a person who empathizes with others can communicate effectively because he is able to interpret the intention or the likely reception of a message correctly.

Effective communication depends on the accurate sending and receiving of non-verbal messages mixed with verbal ones. Whenever we speak with other people, we send and receive nonverbal messages which may support or conflict with the words we use. Nonverbal messages are present whether we speak personally to someone or whether we write to him. Indeed, a formal letter may indicate the desire to establish or remain on a formal level with a person even though the words used might request a casual level. A supervisor who says "Let's just meet informally in my office for a few minutes to discuss your biology class" and then later sits behind his imposing desk as a barrier between the teacher and himself is sending conflicting messages.

The problem of effective communication is summed up well in the quote below:

> *I know that you believe you understand what you think I said, but I am not sure you realize that what you heard is not what I meant.*

A SIMPLE MODEL OF COMMUNICATION

All the complex models of communication which have appeared in the past few years have as their basis a quite simple model. The simplest model involves the concepts of *sender* (that is, source), *channel,* and *receiver* (that is, destination). In diagram form, the model looks like this:

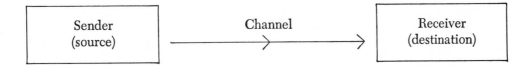

The simplicity of the model is not lost, however, when we add a few embellishments so as to make the model more meaningful. Here we add the concepts of *encoding, decoding,* and *message.* In diagram form the model now looks like this:

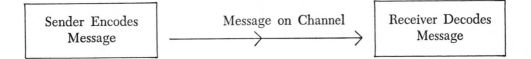

While the message is being *transmitted* on the channel, there can also be *noise* added to it. In this way the receiver receives more than just the message sent. Noise refers to additional information received. Noise makes the correct interpretation of the sender's message more difficult. Also, while the message is on the channel there can be a *loss* of information. That is, the receiver receives only part of the message transmitted by the sender. It is obviously possible to have both noise and loss at the same time. Part of the sender's message may get lost, while at the same time additional outside noise may be added to the remaining part. For example, a student in the back of a large room may not hear all the teacher's words, while at the same time hearing students in the adjoining music room in back of him singing a choral piece.

To show that a person serves both as sender and receiver during communication, it is necessary to make one last slight modification of the model. Even with this change and the addition of the concept of *feedback,* the model remains quite simple. Feedback refers to the sender's perception of how his message is being received and decoded by the receiver. With good feedback the sender can modify his messages in order to effect a more accurate interpretation by the receiver. In diagram form, the model now looks like this:

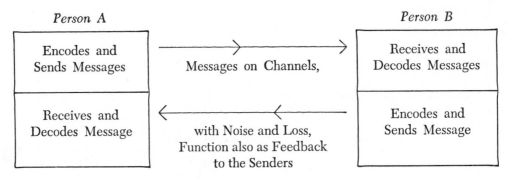

We must keep in mind, in addition to noise and loss, that the correct interpretation of an intended message is hindered by a person's limitations in encoding and decoding. For example, an enraged person finds it difficult to encode, or translate, his ideas into a clear message. Likewise, an angry person finds it difficult to interpret a message correctly because his intense emotional state hinders his decoding ability. Encoding and decoding of a message are affected by a person's emotional state, attitudes, biases, and vantage point.

In light of these many points above,

> *Question:* Is it ever possible to have effective communication with all these interferences?

> *Answer:* Yes, but we must work at it.

AN ACTIVITY TO ILLUSTRATE EFFECTIVE COMMUNICATION

Many people are so familiar with the ideas presented so far in this chapter that they might not feel the importance of the points made concerning the need for open, effective communication between people. The activity presented below is one that we have used many times to forcefully drive home the need for effective communication by demonstrating the results of two types of communication. As a supervisor, you can use this activity with other supervisors, your teachers, or a mixed group of supervisors and teachers.

a. **Step-by-Step Strategy for Conducting the Activity "One-Speaker and Two-Speaker Communication"**

> Step 1. Select a volunteer from the group to serve as sender. Just ask for a volunteer without explaining his task yet to the group or to him.

> Step 2. Ask the sender to study Figure 10-1 for a minute or two. Ask him not to show the figure to anyone. Tell him only that he will be describing the drawing to the group shortly, so that they will draw a similar figure.

> Step 3. Select a volunteer official observer. Tell him that his task will be to observe the sender and the group. (If you wish, select two official observers—one to concentrate on the sender and one to concentrate

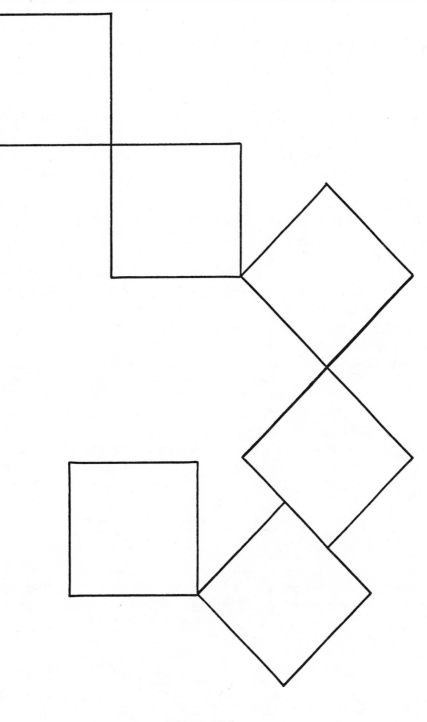

Figure 10-1

on the group.) Ask the observer to take writen notes so he can refer to them later. The observer should note both verbal and nonverbal behavior.

Step 4. Read the following instructions to everyone:

"(*Name of sender*) is going to describe a drawing to you. Listen carefully to his instructions and draw what he describes as accurately as you can. That is, you are to draw what is on the sheet he has. There is no time limit but I will record the time. You may ask no questions of (*Name of sender*). Please do not give audible responses or hints as feedback. Work independently, please."

Step 5. Have the sender sit or stand with his back to the group.

Step 6. Record the time.

Step 7. Ask the sender to begin. While he is describing the figure, be sure there are no audible responses from the group.

Sept 8. Record the time when sender is finished.

Step 9. Ask the group to estimate the accuracy of their drawings. That is, each person should write down next to the figure how many items he estimates he drew correctly in relation to the previous items.

Step 10. Give the sender Figure 10-2 and ask him to study it for a minute or two. Ask him not to show it to anyone.

Step 11. Read the following instructions to everyone:

"(*Name of sender*) is going to describe another drawing to you. This time he will be facing you. You may ask him as many questions as you wish to help you be accurate. He may reply to your questions. In light of your questions, he may amplify any of his statements. But he is not permitted to make any gestures or signals with his hands while describing the drawing. Once again, you are to draw the figure on the sheet he has. There is no time limit but I will record the time as before. Work accurately and independently, please"

Step 12. Have the sender sit or stand facing the group.

Step 13. Record the time.

Step 14. Ask the sender to begin.

Step 15. Record the time when the sender is finished.

Step 16. Ask the group to estimate the accuracy of their drawings. That is, each person should write down next to the figure how many items he estimates he drew correctly in relation to the previous items.

Step 17. Show Figure 10-1 and Figure 10-2 to the group. You can do this best by distributing to each person a reproduction of the two figures. Or, hold up the very same copies the sender used for everyone to see. Or use a large scale poster reproduction, or overhead projection, or chalkboard reproduction.

Step 18. Ask each person to score himself. That is, ask him to write down the number of items for each figure that he actually drew correctly.

Step 19. Fill in the table in Figure 10-3. If it is a small group, you can easily

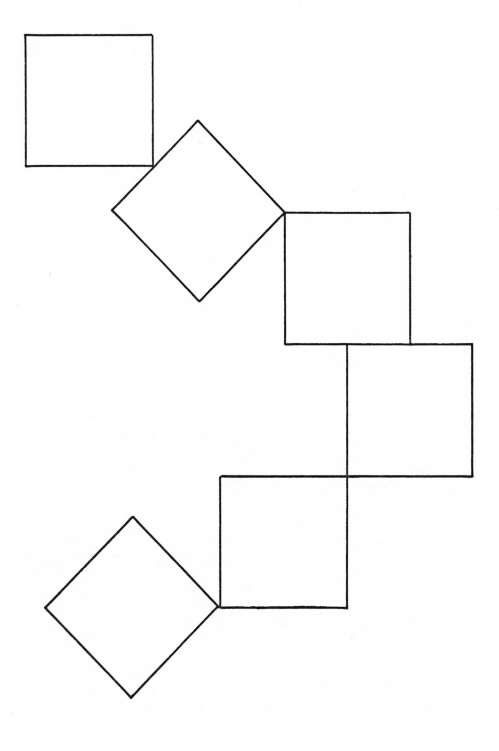

Figure 10-2

Communication Activity

		FIGURE 10-1		FIGURE 10-2	
		# People Estimating Correct	# People Actually Correct	# People Estimating Correct	# People Actually Correct
Number of Items Correct	0				
	1				
	2				
	3				
	4				
	5				
	6				
Total Number of People					
		Took ____ minutes		Took ____ minutes	

Figure 10-3
Communication Activity Table—Blank Form

Communication Activity

		FIGURE 10-1		FIGURE 10-2	
		# People Estimating Correct	# People Actually Correct	# People Estimating Correct	# People Actually Correct
Number of Items Correct	0	0	0	1	0
	1	1	2	1	1
	2	10	13	1	5
	3	14	32	5	4
	4	30	35	7	5
	5	36	19	14	19
	6	13	3	75	70
Total Number of People		104	104	104	104
		Took 6 minutes		Took 8 minutes	

Figure 10-4
Communication Activity Table—Completed Form

fill it in by a quick show of hands. If the group is large, ask each sub-group of 6 to 8 people to fill out its own table. Then by combining the tables of the several sub-groups you can easily create a master table for the entire group.

Step 20. Show the completed table to everyone.

Step 21. Begin debriefing this activity.

    a. Ask the official observer to give his report.

    b. Ask the group to make its own observations based on their experience, the report of the official observer, and the data presented in the completed table. The following questions should serve as the focus for the discussion:

       1. Which figure took longer to complete?

       2. On which figure were you more accurate?

       3. Qn which figure did you estimate higher?

       4. What other observations can you make from the data in the completed table?

       5. How did you feel during this activity (sender and group)?

       6. What generalizations can you make based on all these data?

       7. Based on these data and other experiences you have had in similar situations, what general statements can you offer?

       8. What implications do you see for education based on all of these comments?

       9. What steps can you take in your job to bring about effective 2-speaker communication?

Obviously, you need not ask a question if someone else asks it of the group or raises the point of the question himself during the discussion. Just direct the group's attention to the point made.

b. Making the Point: Illustrative Results from Using this Activity

We have used this activity with many groups of educators. Let us, therefore, look at some illustrative results from several groups so that you can better understand the activity and know what to expect when you conduct it yourself.

Figure 10-4 is the completed table from a very large group of teachers. These results are similar to those of every other group, large or small, which has done this activity. Even without additional comments by the official observers, the group members, and the sender these results are powerful and meaningful. Look them over and jot down at least three ideas you see in the data.

1. _____

2. _____

3. _____

Below are some of the comments the teachers made during the debriefing session.

Yes, even with this large a group of 107 people (1 sender + 2 official observers + 104 group members) the debriefing session was possible and meaningful because we first had sub-group (6 people) debriefings and then a whole group debriefing.

1. Official observer I: I noticed that the group was seriously doing the activity both times. But on Figure 10-1 some were looking around at their neighbor's sheets for help. Even those who weren't cheating look frustrated on Figure 10-1. Marian (the sender) was nervous. She fidgeted with the paper and her voice seemed nervous, too. On Figure 10-2, there was hardly any cheating. Once Mary asked the first question we had a stream of questions. Marian wasn't nervous at all. She answered each question carefully and even checked to see if the answer was clear. My first impression as I walked around was that the group was doing better, and they did as you can see in the table.

2. Official observer II: I just want to add one thing or two, since my notes are almost the same as Joe's. The group seemed to really move when they realized they could ask questions to clear up the figure they were drawing. Also, the group was frustrated with Figure 10-1, but so was Marian. They both were.

3. Group:

   a. Figure 10-2 took longer than Figure 10-1, but more people were more accurate.

   b. In Figure 10-2, the estimates and the actual were close together. In Figure 10-1, the estimates and actual weren't so close, not nearly as close as in Figure 10-2.

   c. In Figure 10-1, the group clusters around 3 and 4 correct and then slides off on both sides. In Figure 10-2, the group clusters around 6 corect with sudden drops to 5 and 4 correct.

   d. In Figure 10-1, the confidence level is fairly high but the results don't warrant it. The confidence level in Figure 10-2 is higher and the results warrant it.

   e. We felt better when we knew we could ask questions, and then we did ask questions.

   f. Even though I didn't ask a question, I benefited from someone else's question.

   g. It helped when Marian (sender) repeated and tried other explanations as soon as she realized we were in trouble.

   h. I felt better because I felt that Marian (sender) felt better with Figure 10-2.

   i. When you have a 2-way conversation, everything seems to improve—accuracy, confidence, congruence between idea and behavior.

   j. This shows you the need for participation by the group. Like in teaching, if the students participate and talk to the teacher rather than just sitting there, then it's better for everyone—teacher and students both.

   k. We missed some visual props in Figure 10-1 and Figure 10-2. We think that the results would even be better if Marian (sender) could have used the board or her hands or something. Just talking wasn't enough. We missed the visual non-verbal stuff.

4. Sender: I really was frustrated with Figure 10-1, since I had no way of knowing how I was doing. That bugged me. I couldn't get feedback. But on Figure 10-2, I felt better 'cause I got feedback from their questions and their faces. I didn't mind all the

questions too much since I thought it was helping. Now that it's over I really feel better.

Summary and Synthesis of the Points of this Communication Activity

From the data and comments of the teacher in this group, and other groups as well, it is possible to alert you to many points about communication.

When people have 2-speaker communication, the accuracy of the communication goes up, the confidence of the communicators goes up, and so does the amount of time used. There is also a better match between estimate and actual behavior. There are better feelings about the communication, too.

One-way communication is faster, but the communicators are less accurate, less confident, and less congruent. Some people do all right with 1-speaker communication, but most do better when they are actively involved in the task before them. The verbal aspect of communication needs to be supplemented by the non-verbal aspect, which can clarify the sender's message. We need both verbal and non-verbal in our attempt to have effective communication.

The implications are many. We must provide adequate time to communicate. If not, we will go too fast and not achieve what we hope to. We must so set up the situation to allow and encourage questions from the receivers so they can clarify their own problems. (1) This is especially important for the *classroom* teaching situation, since we know that there are too few student questions all too often. (2) It is also important in *supervision,* where the teacher may already be leaning to ineffective communication because of tension and nervous strain.

A VARIATION OF THE COMMUNICATION ACTIVITY WHICH EMPHASIZES THE NEED FOR MORE PRECISE LANGUAGE COMMON TO THE COMMUNICATORS

For those who wish to spend a bit more time (about 20 more minutes) in order to make another important point regarding effective communication, there is an interesting variation on the communication activity.

This variation is designed to make the point that communicators generally do better when they have a precise language to depend on between them. When the sender and the receiver have a preestablished helpful language system that they have agreed upon, the accuracy of the message increases.

a. Step-by-Step Strategy for Conducting this Variation

The steps of this variation are the same as the basic activity through Step 16 and begin right after that:

Step 1 through Step 16. The same as before.

Step 16A. Tell the sender and the group that there will be another figure like the others. This time, however, their task is to devise a special system, that is, a language, so they can communicate easily (even 1-way.) (The group will probably come up with such ideas as labeling the points of the square, indicating the tilt of the square by giving the degrees of the angle size, by calling a square a diamond when it stands on a point rather than a side, and so forth.)

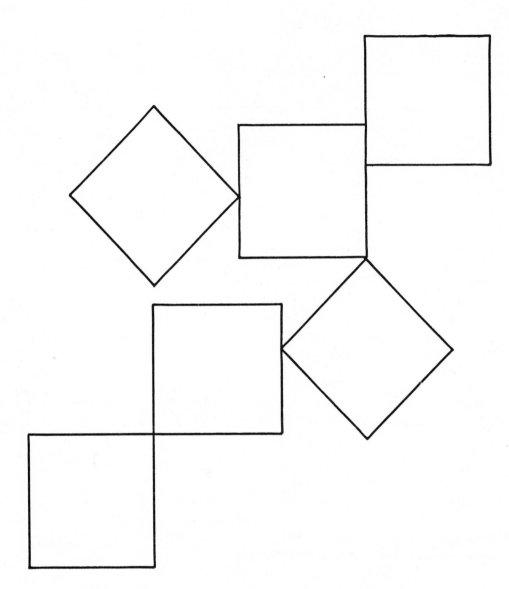

Figure 10-5

Step 16B. The sender can serve as the leader of the discussion for devising the system. Or, the group can select its own leader. The sender and the group together devise their own system of terms and their own strategy. (About 10-15 minutes.)

Step 16C. Give the sender Figure 10-5 and ask him to study it for a minute or two. Ask him not to show it to anyone.

Step 16D. Read the following instructions to everyone: "(*Name of sender*) is going to describe another drawing to you. Use the special system of communication which you all have devised. As before, draw the figure as accurately as you can. There is no time limit, but I will record the time. Please do not give audible responses or hints as feedback. Work accurately and independently, please."

Step 16E. Have the sender sit or stand with his back to the group.

Step 16F. Record the time.

Step 16G. Ask the sender to begin, using the special system of communication. While he is describing the figure, be sure there is no audible response from the group.

Step 16H. Record the time when the sender is finished.

Step 17 through Step 21. The same as before but remember to show all 3 figures in Step 17, Figure 10-1, Figure 10-2, and Figure 10-5. In Step 19 use the expanded table in Figure 10-6 in order to include data on Figure 10-5.

Communication Activity

		FIGURE 10-1		FIGURE 10-2		FIGURE 10-5	
		# People Estimating Correct	# People Actually Correct	# People Estimating Correct	# People Actually Correct	# People Estimating Correct	# People Actually Correct
Number of Items Correct	0						
	1						
	2						
	3						
	4						
	5						
	6						
Total Number of People							
		Took _____ minutes		Took _____ minutes		Took _____ minutes	

Figure 10-6
Communication Activity Table—Blank Form

b. Making the Point: Illustrative Results from Using this Variation

In general, the results of this variation are the same as the basic activity. You can see this by examining the completed tables on the next few pages. What is different is the *added* result emphasizing the use of a precise, common-to-all language system to facilitate the communication.

On the next page are the completed tables (Figure 10-7 and 10-8) from two small groups of people. These results are similar to those of every other group, large or small, which has done this variation activity. Even without the additional comments by the official observer, the group members, and the sender, these results are meaningful. Look both tables over and jot down at least three ideas you see in the data.

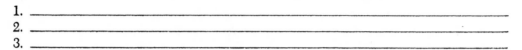

The results (Figure 10-7) of the first group, a group of young interns in the Newark, New Jersey Public Schools, are quite similar to the results (Figure 10-8) of the second group, a mixed group of teachers and supervisors from several central New Jersey school systems. In each case Figure 10-5 took less time than Figure 10-2, but more than Figure 10-1. In each case the accuracy in terms of all 6 items correct was better in Figure 10-5. Overall, the second group did better in Figure 10-5. The first group slipped a bit in accuracy for everything below 6 correct in Figure 10-5, compared with Figure 10-2.

Both made similar comments in the debriefing sessions. They pointed out that the special system helped them in their accuracy and confidence with 1-direction communication. They were both impressed by the decrease in time and the increase of accuracy over Figure 10-2 at the top level of Figure 10-5. But they were amazed at the fantastic difference between Figure 10-1 and Figure 10-5, both 1-direction communication patterns.

This point is particularly important in light of our previous chapters, Chapters 4, 5, 6, and 7, presenting systems for observing classroom teaching. With a special system that is known to all, it is possible to make a move toward effective communication.

ALTERNATE FIGURES FOR THIS COMMUNICATION ACTIVITY

If, for some reason, you do not particularly like squares (as shown in Figures 10-1, 2 & 5), three alternative figures appear in the next few pages. Figures 10-9, 10, & 11 can be used interchangeably with those presented earlier. They offer a little variety and are particularly good if you plan to use the variation suggested, since the participants will need a special system to deal with circles and triangles as well as squares.

APPLICATION OF THE MESSAGE

The leader of this communication activity has the potential of leading his faculty to apply the points raised by the group in the debriefing session. If you conduct this

Communication Activity

Number of Items Correct	FIGURE 10-1		FIGURE 10-2		FIGURE 10-5	
	# People Estimating Correct	# People Actually Correct	# People Estimating Correct	# People Actually Correct	# People Estimating Correct	# People Actually Correct
0	3	1	1	0	2	1
1	2	3	0	0	0	1
2	2	4	1	1	3	3
3	7	4	3	2	2	2
4	3	5	2	4	3	3
5	1	3	7	6	5	1
6	4	2	8	9	7	11
Total Number of People	22	22	22	22	22	22
	Took 6 minutes		Took 12 minutes		Took 7 minutes	

Figure 10-7
Communication Activity Table—Completed Form

Communication Activity

Number of Items Correct	FIGURE 10-1		FIGURE 10-2		FIGURE 10-5	
	# People Estimating Correct	# People Actually Correct	# People Estimating Correct	# People Actually Correct	# People Estimating Correct	# People Actually Correct
0	0	0	1	1	0	0
1	2	2	0	1	0	0
2	1	3	1	0	0	0
3	6	7	4	3	4	2
4	3	5	2	1	2	2
5	9	3	3	4	3	5
6	0	1	10	11	12	12
Total Number of People	21	21	21	21	21	21
	Took 5½ minutes		Took 13 minutes		Took 11 minutes	

Figure 10-8
Communication Activity Table—Completed Form

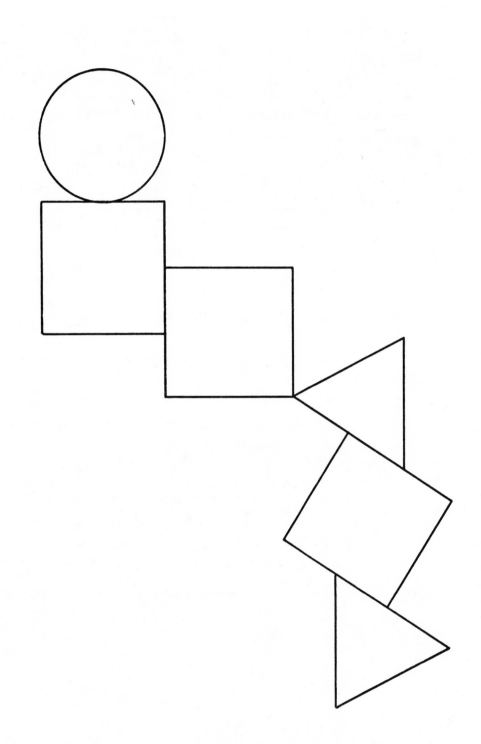

Figure 10-9

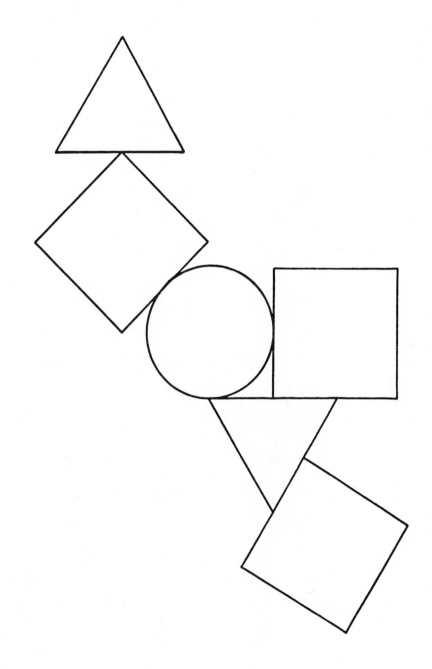

Figure 10-10

175

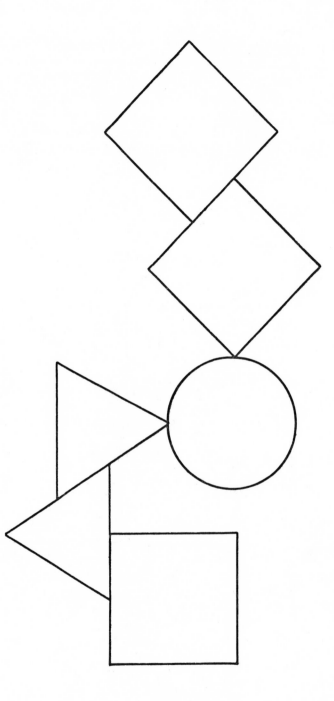

Figure 10-11

activity with teachers, then you can direct the discussion and application to classroom teaching, supervision, or general school affairs. If you conduct this activity with other supervisors, then you can direct the discussion to the supervision process as well as general school affairs. If the group is mixed with teachers and supervisors, then you can focus on either teaching or supervision depending on your need.

If you have time after conducting the communication activity, you can immediately launch into an application session. (See Question #9 in the debriefing Step 21 listed previously.) Since usually there is not much more time available, you should plan for an application session afterwards.

The application session should begin with a few excerpts from the debriefing discussion, with identification of the people who made these interesting remarks. Then, there should be a listing of some of the important points made by the faculty. Probably they will be similar to the ones listed in this chapter under *Making the Point*. The procedure will refresh everyone's memory, give the faculty something to focus on, and give you an opportunity to select those messages you particularly want your faculty to attend to. A sample summary sheet (Figure 10-12) follows on the next page, and a sample completed one (Figure 10-13) follows it as a guide. Look them over carefully to note the points raised.

The application session should aim to push forward. If several sub-groups seem particularly interested in different aspects of communication, then you can break the faculty up into small task groups. If the decision is to focus on only one key issue, then the group can proceed as a whole or break up into small groups. In any case, you should direct the faculty to work on specific changes in what they do.

    A. Direct them to be specific.
    B. Request some "Do's"—positive things to do. Emphasize this part strongly.
    C. Request some (but do not emphasize) "Don'ts"—negative things to eliminate.

If you want to try more than the usual type of application session, try BRAIN-STORMING to get new fresh ideas. See Chapter 12 for suggestions on How to Utilize Brainstorming with Your Faculty.

SKILLS FOR IMPROVING COMMUNICATION

Once we are aware of the importance of effective communication and how the various factors of feedback, involvement, time, confidence, and a special common language affect communication, then we also need to take steps to improve our communication skills. There are several basic skills which everyone can develop and maintain so that he can communicate effectively with others. The supervisors can utilize these skills when he communicates with other educators, students, and parents. He can also teach these skills to his teachers so that they can improve their communication skills.

a. Listening

Listening is a critical skill in communication. Perhaps it is the most important skill for you as a supervisor, as you seek to understand and help your teachers. You

TO: _____

FROM: _____

RE: *Follow-up from the "One-Speaker and Two-Speaker Communication Activity"*

    Led by _____ on _____, 19_____.

1. *Quotable quotes from the session:*

    A.

    B.

    C.

2. *Key points raised:*

    A.

    B.

    C.

3. *Decisions to follow through for implementation:*

Figure 10-12
Summary Sheet for One-Speaker and Two-Speaker Communication Activity—Blank Form

TO: *Faculty*

FROM: *Pat Robinson*

RE: *Follow-up from the "One-Speaker and Two-Speaker Communication Activity"*

Led by ____me____ on ____August 28____, 19____.

1. *Quotable quotes from the session:*

   A. Bill Meisner, "It's just like in a formal lecture compared with a seminar discussion. It's true."

   B. Ila Martin, "I think I need some help in communicating better."

   C. Marina Berkowitz, "It was so frustrating not to be able to ask a question."

2. *Key points raised:*

   A. We need feedback to communicate effectively.

   B. Accuracy and confidence increase with 2-way communication.

   C. We probably all need to sharpen our communication skills.

3. *Decisions to follow through for implementation:*

   We could profit from suggestions on how to incorporate the learning of effective communication skills into our students curriculum and our in-service workshop programs as well. Please make suggestions individually or by teams for all of us to consider at next week's meeting.

Figure 10-13
**Summary Sheet for One-Speaker and Two-Speaker Communication Activity—
Completed Form**

need to show the teacher that you are willing to receive a message from him. Unless the teacher feels that the lines of communication are open between you, he is not likely to talk. Just being silent is not enough for you to do. The teacher must perceive that your silence is a sign of readiness to listen rather than an opportunity to daydream. You can signal your openness to reception by:

1. facing the teacher.
2. sitting or standing near the teacher.
3. leaning or bending slightly toward the teacher.
4. focusing on the teacher's eyes or slightly below them.
5. not interrupting the teacher in order to best him with a retort.

A simple, but effective, non-verbal technique is to count 5 seconds after the teacher stops before you begin to talk. This pause will indicate that you have not just been sitting and waiting desperately to talk, that you are now considering his words before you proceed, and that you still offer him the opportunity to continue if he wishes to. Another non-verbal technique is for you to take some notes. Note taking will keep you physically active and mentally alert, as well as signal the teacher that you consider his message important enough to write it down so you can remember it.

The most explicit way of telling the teacher that you are listening is to say so. You can simply say, "I'm listening. Please go ahead and talk to me." You can also "tell," in a non-verbal way, that you are listening by the very manner you talk to the teacher. That is to say, your words carry the non-verbal message that you are listening attentively. To clarify and specify this point of demonstrating that you are listening, let us turn to the next four basic skills.

b. Paraphrasing

When you paraphrase what another person says, you restate the essence of his message in a short, capsule form. You use his words, plus some of your own, to indicate that you have understood him and *to clarify to both of you* the meaning of the message sent. When you paraphrase a teacher's remarks, you indicate that you

1. are listening to him.
2. have understood him.
3. care about him.
4. wish to respond with an accurate idea of his message.

You can lead into a paraphrasing with such phrases as:

1. Do you mean . . .
2. Do I understand correctly that . . .
3. I read you that . . .
4. In short, you're saying that . . .
5. The essence of your point is that . .
6. Are you saying that . . .

One simple technique for practicing this skill of paraphrasing is to set yourself this goal when you confer with a teacher or teachers: speak your own thoughts only after you have paraphrased the previous speaker's message. You can even add one condition to this if you wish to: speak your own thoughts only after you have paraphrased the previous speaker's message *to his satisfaction*. If you have done a good job by paraphrasing, according to the previous speaker, then speak your own thoughts. If, however, the previous speaker is not satisfied with your paraphrasing, request him to clarify to you the meaning of his message.

Try it.

c. Perception Checking

When you check your perception of another person, you indicate your interpretation of his feelings and beliefs. Whereas paraphrasing deals with the cognitive aspect of the message received, perception checking concentrates on the affective dimension. You check not so much the words of the message, but the tone and the "hidden agenda" of the message. Since this involves an interpretation of feelings and emotions, it is best stated in a tentative manner.

You can lead into a check of your perceptions with such phrases as:

1. You seem to be . . .
2. I get the impression that you are . . .
3. You appear to be . . .
4. It sounds to me like you are . . .
5. From here it seems like you are . . .

You can complete the above examples with comments about the teacher being tense, overwhelmed, angry, satisfied, happy, or interested. The point here is to be tentative, and you can show this by following up with a question like: "Is this so?"

If you utilize this basic communication skill, you will demonstrate, as with paraphrasing, that you are listening, understanding, caring, and responding accurately. You can use this skill at all times, but especially in a conversation that is emotionally loaded and challenging to the participants. You can use it, as with paraphrasing, before you speak your own thoughts. Try it.

d. Adjusting Level

When you adjust the level of your communication, you go up and down the ladder of abstraction so as to make your message clear to the other person. You adjust your level from concrete to abstract so as to clarify your thoughts to someone. You do so as you read the feedback from him sent to you verbally and non-verbally. When you adjust your level you indicate that you are heeding the messages sent to you. Whereas listening, paraphrasing, and perception checking are primarily your function as a communication receiver, the skill of adjusting level moves you to the sender side of the communication flow. But you still function as a receiver because, in order to adjust your level properly, you must be listening carefully, too.

You demonstrate your mobility on the communication ladder when you adjust from the abstract to the concrete and vice versa. For example, if you are talking about "goal setting," which is abstract, you can shift to "moving 5 points on the warmth dimension of the Tuckman Form" (see the chapter on Improving Classroom Climate), which is concrete. By giving specifics for abstractions and by abstracting the general meaning from specifics, you continually adjust your level so as to be clear to the teacher you supervise. When you restate your point with an adjustment of level, you add "redundance" to the communication, and this helps the receiver to interpret your message accurately.

One simple technique is to try to give two specifics for every abstraction used and an abstraction for every cluster of specifics. Try it.

e. Behavior Description

When you describe behavior of another person, you communicate what happened specifically. You describe to the person what he did, not what you think or inferred were his intentions, not what you think were his motives, and not sweeping generalizations about him. For example, you say to a teacher, "Today you asked 15 questions in ten minutes." Behavior description reduces the amount and degree of inferring that you do. It keeps you from assigning a motive to the teacher which he may reject. It keeps you with the immediate past. In keeping yourself with specific behavior, you facilitate good communication. This is so since the assignment of motives and making of generalizations about a person often lead to ineffective communication because they encourage defensiveness.

Behavior description is an important skill for a supervisor. Indeed, in the earlier chapters dealing with observation, the thrust there was to provide frameworks for you so that you will have the language to use in describing behavior meaningfully to the teacher. When the teacher receives a meaningful description of his behavior, then he has the material with which to draw his own generalizations, plan his own steps for change, or investigate his own motives. In any case, it is more helpful for the teacher to receive descriptions than inferences about what he did.

FURTHER SUGGESTIONS ON EFFECTIVE COMMUNICATION

There is no doubt that, in this complex and sensitive area of supervision, we need to strive toward better and better communication. We can improve as we aim to communicate effectively. It will help us if our teachers are aware of the problems of communication and the effects of certain factors. A supervisor can alert his teachers to the need for effective exchange by conducting the communication activity, with or without the variation presented in this chapter. The activity will sensitize the teachers quickly to the need for effective communication in teaching and in supervision.

The supervisor can facilitate effective exchange by practicing the 5 basic skills presented here plus any other personal ones he has developed. He can teach these to his teachers so that they can practice them in their communications, too. These 5 Communications Skills of

1. Listening
2. Paraphrasing
3. Perception Checking
4. Adjusting Level
5. Behavior Description

can be Supplemented by these Further Suggestions:

1. Keep your *messages*, all the verbal and nonverbal ones, *congruent* with each other and your behavior.
2. *Increase* the *redundancy* of your message by repeating key points and using non-verbal and verbal aspects to supplement each other, as well as by paraphrasing, perception checking, and adjusting level.
3. *Establish* and maintain *trust and warmth* with your colleagues so that you are a credible communicator.
4. Make sure that the *facts* you raise are *accurate* and the ideas you present are reasonable, so that people will accept you as believable and trustworthy.
5. Be *open about the intentions* of your message.
6. Take *personal responsibility* for your messages. You can show this explicitly by using the pronouns *I, my, mine,* and *me* to indicate personal involvement.

With these skills and supplementary suggestions you can facilitate effective communication.

Chapter 11

How to Use a Simulation Game with Your Faculty

185

How to Use A Simulation Game with Your Faculty

INTRODUCTION AND OBJECTIVES

Without a doubt, the fastest growing area in the field of education is simulation games. Simulation advocates have been around since the Egyptians made dolls for their children, but it is only in recent times that educators have turned to the use of simulation as a legitimate, acceptable approach across the entire spectrum of education—teaching, supervision, and administration.

With this in mind, in this chapter, we shall briefly present (1) the advantages of simulation, (2) an actual simulation activity that has proven most successful in developing an excellent foundation for a sound supervisory relationship, and (3) an approach for following up the simulation activity.

At the conclusion of this chapter, the reader should be able to:

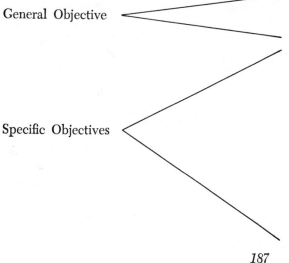

General Objective

Specific Objectives

1. Understanding the role and potential of using a simulation game with his/her faculty.

2. Define a simulation game as applied to supervision.

3. List at least 3 advantages of utilizing a simulation game in supervision.

4. Conduct the suggested simulation game with confidence with his/her staff by following the step-by-step strategy presented.

5. Know how to follow up the simulation meeting with an application session.

DEFINITIONS AND ADVANTAGES OF SIMULATION GAME

Simulations are operating imitations of real situations or objects. A simulation is a working model that replicates essential features in real life. Dolls, toy airplanes, and model cars like the famous car and truck Match Box series are *simple simulations.* The Link pilot trainers of World War II fame, the weightless moon laboratory at Cape Kennedy for the astronauts, and the machines used in automobile driving centers are complex, *sophisticated simulations of objects and processes.*

A simulation game is more than just a simulation. It is a combination of a simulation and a game. In a simulation game, players become decision-makers, act out the simulated social process, and make the system "go" according to specified goals, resources, and rules.

Examples of some very popular simulation games, which most of us have played at one time or another are:

1. Playing *house.*
2. Playing *cops and robbers.*
3. Playing *Monopoly.*
4. Playing *school.*
5. Playing *doctor.*
6. Playing *chess.* (Yes, even chess, an encirclement game, originally was a simulation of war with medieval names and relative power roles for the various pieces.)

Recently, games advocates have taken to using simulations in supervision. The *advantages* of using a simulation game in supervision are clear.

1. Simulation is natural. Much of what we learned as children we learned through simulation. Everyone is accustomed to a simulation game simply because he has experienced it before. Any specific simulated situation may be new, indeed, but the overall idea of letting loose to pretend that something-is-what-it-is-not is old hat.
2. Simulation games facilitate interaction among teachers and supervisors. People are encouraged to communicate with and, hence, learn from the others during the simulation. Peer learning is accomplished, and this is often the strongest learning a leader can provide. Much of what a supervisor would like to say to his teachers he can say easily in a simulation game, since the context is facilitative. Polarization between supervisor and teachers is removed. Furthermore, teachers will teach each other and help each other toward creating a healthy supervision atmosphere.
3. Simulation games motivate teachers and supervisors because there is fun involved and interest is high.
4. Simulation games are economical. In a short period of time, supervisors can get at essential elements of good supervision.
5. Simulation games offer a welcome break from the conventional approach to supervision, which often is dull and/or threatening.

6. Simulation games bring out their messages with significant power. The impact of the message is powerful and noticeable.

The great Greek philosopher and educator, Socrates, recognized these advantages when he said, "Train them by a kind of game, and you will be able to see more clearly the natural bent of each."

AN ACTUAL, EFFECTIVE, EASILY USED SIMULATION GAME

What follows (Fig. 11-1) is a simulation game, which we designed and have used successfully many times with supervisors and teachers.
"The Cousin's Choice: Fake or Real"

1. The scenario.
2. Strategy for conducting this simulation.
3. Suggestions and comments.

STEP-BY-STEP STRATEGY FOR CONDUCTING THIS SIMULATION GAME

Step 1. Warm up the group with a friendly greeting and statement that they will be involved in a simulation activity called "The Cousin's Choice: Fake or Real."

Step 2. Distribute the sheet describing the situation. Go over the situation with the group so that everyone understands the scenario.

Step 3. Explain the inheritance rewards for each of the four possible combinations of fake identity and real identity for the two persons involved.

> Person #1 Fake and Person #2 Fake
> Person #1 Fake and Person #2 Real
> Person #1 Real and Person #2 Fake
> Person #1 Real and Person #2 Real

You might well ask someone in the group to restate the various rewards to check your explanation. Do not get bogged down here. Be clear and move on. Clarity will come as the activity progresses.

Step 4. Ask participants to pair off and sit back to back. Pairs should move their chairs around so that they sit comfortably back to back.
(Before you begin this step, designate one person as your extra "odd" player. He should not pair off immediately, but should wait to see if he is needed. If there is an even number of players without him, designate him as the official game observer. If there is an odd number of players without him, then he plays as the partner of the leftover player.)

Step 5. Announce the rules.
A. No talking or writing to each other until permitted by the leader.
B. Each participant privately decides for a fake identity or a real

THE COUSIN'S CHOICE: FAKE OR REAL

Situation

A wealthy, eccentric person died suddenly, leaving a large amount of money in a will. When the lawyers opened the bank vault to read the will, they found the following terms among others:

A. One million dollars ($1,000,000) to be divided equally among surviving nephews or nieces.
B. If no nephews or nieces survive, then $50,000 for each surviving first cousin and the rest to charity.
C. If only one surviving heir is eligible to take under the will, then $750,000 to this heir and $250,000 to charity

You are one of two first cousins who come to town to claim under the will. You two are the only heirs to appear before the lawyers to claim your inheritance, but you have no time to talk to each other. You each separately read a copy of the will and realize that nephews or nieces receive substantially more than cousins. You each have the choice to claim your real identity as a cousin of the deceased, or to claim a fake identity as a nephew or niece of the deceased. Neither of you is aware of the other's choice. Your decision will be very much affected by a prediction of your cousin's choice on identity .

Inheritance

1. If you both claim a fake identity and support each other, you each get $500,000 but must leave your present life and live in a far away place as a nephew (niece) of the deceased.
2. If you both claim your real identity, then you each get $50,000.
3. If one of you claims your real identity and one claims a fake identity, then the "real" cousin gets $750,000 and the "fake" nephew (niece) gets $0. This is so because the "real" cousin will testify in court against the "fake" nephew (niece), and the court will believe the cousin. The "fake" nephew (niece) therefore gets $0, because he claimed falsely and is ineligible to take under the will. He is also subject to punishment by the court. The real cousin gets $750,000 as the sole surviving heir eligible to take under the will.

Figure 11-1
Simulation Game Scenario

The Cousin's Choice: Fake or Real

RECORD SHEET

	My choice	Other's choice	My inheritance	Other's inheritance
1				
2				
3				
4				
5				
6				
7				
8				
9				
10				

Figure 11-2
Simulated Game Record Sheet—Blank Form

The Cousin's Choice: Fake or Real
(Person A after 10 decisions)

RECORD SHEET

	My choice	Other's choice	My inheritance	Other's inheritance
1	fake	real	$ 0	$ 750,000
2	fake	real	0	750,000
3	real	real	50,000	50,000
4	real	real	50,000	50,000
5	real	real	50,000	50,000
6	fake	real	0	750,000
7	real	real	50,000	50,000
8	real	real	50,000	50,000
9	real	real	50,000	50,000
10	real	real	50,000	50,000

Figure 11-3
Simulation Game Record Sheet—Completed Form

identity. He writes his decision on a piece of scrap paper. All he writes is "fake" or "real."

C. Goal of this activity is: "Do the best you can." State the goal this way. Say this and nothing more.

Step 6. Ask group to make its first decision. Each player should write his decision on a piece of paper and pass the paper over his shoulder to his partner. Remind the players not to talk to each other.

Step 7. Distribute the Record Sheet now. Ask players to fill in the first row. Check to see that everyone understands how to fill in the record sheet properly. (By distributing the Record Sheet now, you simplify the procedure, taking one thing at its appropriate time. Also, it is better for participants to learn that they will record and repeat the process only after they make at least one decision.) See Figure 11-3.

Step 8. Ask group to continue this procedure nine more times, for a total of ten times. Clearly announce that each person may decide for a fake or real identity during each decision time, since each is independent of the others. Remind the group that the pattern is: write decision; pass paper; and record decision. The partners are not to write and record more than one decision at a time. All they need to write is "fake" or "real." They may use the same pieces of scrap paper, if they wish, by simply crossing out the previous decisions when they write their new decisions.

Step 9.   When the players have all finished deciding and recording 10 times, ask the partners now to face each other and talk together for 3–5 minutes. Direct them to talk about what happened, based on the Situation and Inheritance Sheet and their filled in Record Sheets.

Step 10.   After 3–5 minutes, ask partners to sit back to back again, not to talk to each other, and to repeat the above procedure 10 more times for a grand total of 20 times. Remind them to write decisions, pass their slips of paper, and record their decisions *one at a time*. No talking when they are finished.

You may distribute a new copy of the record sheet to everyone if you wish. Or, you can simply ask everyone to extend the lines of the completed record sheet he has downward to make room for this new cycle. (Make sure you go up to 20 decisions. Do not cut this short. Our experience is that players do need the next 10 decisions. By distributing the new record sheet now or by extending the old one now, the players do not know ahead of time that they will go up to 20 decisions. And this is what should be when the partners talk to each other after the 10th decision.) See Figure 11-4 which follows.

Step 11.   When the players have all finished recording the 20th decision, ask each person to write on a piece of paper at least 3 adjectives, terms, or phrases to describe his impression of his partner during the activity. He should consider only what he thinks of his partner during the game, and discount everything he knows about his partner prior to the activity. In other words, each person will be completing the sentence, "My partner was ——————," at least three times.

The players do this while they are still sitting back to back, and before any more talking begins. See the examples which follow.

EXAMPLES OF ADJECTIVES OFTEN USED AS PART OF STEP 11

greedy	afraid
consistent	trusting
"rat"	stupid
trustworthy	agreeable
honest	easily convinced
nice	liar
fair	shrewd
wise	selfish
generous	unscrupulous
giving	moral
cautious	dishonest-to-the-law but honest-to-his-partner

The Cousin's Choice: Fake or Real

(Person B after 20 decisions)

RECORD SHEET

	My choice	Other's choice	My inheritance	Other's inheritance
1	real	fake	$750,000	$ 0
2	real	fake	$ 750,000	0
3	real	real	50,000	$ 50,000
4	real	real	50,000	50,000
5	real	real	50,000	50,000
6	real	fake	750,000	50,000
7	real	real	50,000	50,000
8	real	real	50,000	50,000
9	real	real	50,000	50,000
10	real	real	50,000	50,000
11	real	real	50,000	50,000
12	real	real	50,000	50,000
13	real	real	50,000	50,000
14	real	real	50,000	50,000
15	real	real	50,000	50,000
16	real	real	50,000	50,000
17	real	real	50,000	50,000
18	real	real	50,000	50,000
19	real	real	50,000	50,000
20	real	real	50,000	50,000

Figure 11-4
Simulation Game Record Sheet—With 20 Decisions—Completed Form

Step 12. When they are finished, ask the players to face each other, exchange these papers, and talk about their decisions and impressions of each other.

Step 13. After a few minutes, begin to debrief. The debriefing is an absolute must for this simulation game. It provides the opportunity to interpret what happened and to learn from the activity. Allow adequate time for debriefing.

    a. Begin the debriefing by encouraging the group to talk simply about what happened during the simulation. This will review the simulation and provide a foundation of data upon which to build in order to analyze, interpret, and learn from the game. It will loosen up the group and get them talking, since it is easy to talk on this concrete, non-threatening level. That is, ask such questions as: "What decisions did you make, fake or real? Who decided to give his real identity? Who decided to give a fake identity? Who switched somewhere during the 20 times? What led you to decide as you did? What adjectives did you use to describe your partner? Is your partner's description of you accurate? If not, how would you describe yourself during the simulation activity? What did you talk about during the 3–5 minute conversation between the 10th and 11th decision? What effect did the conversation have on your subsequent decisions?"

    b. Encourage the group to talk about how they felt during the activity, about their beliefs and feelings. Ask such questions as: "How did you feel when you decided to give a fake identity? How did you feel when you decided to give a real identity? Why did you decide to be fake? Why did you decide to be real? If your partner broke an agreement with you and switched a decision (that is, double-crossed you), how did you feel? Did you feel like getting even with him?"

    c. Encourage the group to talk about who they are. This is an important feature of this simulation game. Ask such questions as: "Are you a trusting person? Acquisitive (money hungry)? Competitive? Honest? Trustworthy? Do you want to be someone else? Would you be someone else if you received enough money? Are you cautious? Daring? Risky? Who are you really? Are you a fake?"

    d. Discuss the similarities between this simulation game and their real lives as teachers and supervisors. The drawing of parallels with the real world of education is the central feature of this simulation game. Ask such questions as: "In what ways are your activities as a teacher or supervisor like your activity in this simulation game? What key ideas does this simulation give us about teaching? What key ideas does this simulation give us about supervision?"

    e. Encourage the group to discuss future activities for building upon their experiences with this simulation game. Ask such questions as: In what ways can we change our classroom activities as a result of what we have learned from playing this simulation game? In what way can we change our supervision procedures as a result of what we have learned from playing this simulation game?"

Step 14. Summarize, generalize and conclude. At various spots, but especially at the end, there is a great need for summarizing, generalizing, and concluding. The generalizations and conclusions constitute the learning which arises from this simulation game. The leader can do this task himself, if he so chooses. Better yet, he should request the group to list first some key ideas that have come forth during the discussion, then to offer some generalizations based on these ideas, and finally to draw some conclusions. This latter approach is more effective. If you use the latter approach, the generalizations and conclusions will be more meaningful since they come from the group itself. You can set off this process by asking each person to complete whichever of the following sentences you feel is more appropriate:

a. Based on this simulation, I realize about teaching that ＿＿＿＿＿.

b. Based on this simulation, I realize about supervision that ＿＿＿＿.

Be sure to ask the group to share their completed sentences.

Step 15. Move forward. Before leaving this simulation game behind, structure the activity so that you launch yourself and the group into something new built on this simulation game. In this way, you bridge current activity with future activity while interest is high. For example, you might schedule your next meeting as a time to plan and implement ideas. Suggest that you will provide a summary just to get the meeting off to a good start. See the *Application* section later in this chapter for further ideas.

SUGGESTIONS AND COMMENTS

1. Before playing this game with your faculty, try it out with a few select friends just to get the hang of it. Try it as a social, parlor game at your home. All you need is a minimum of six players to gain experience. Besides getting the feel of the game, you will have a fun evening with your friends. This tryout session is especially suggested to you if you have little previous experience with simulation.

2. Please follow the given strategy at least the first few times. It will give you support. It is one that has proven successful many times already. Once you are comfortable with the game, feel free to modify anything and everything to fit your needs.

3. You can conduct the entire game in 1¼ hours if you play rapidly. If you have more time, you can go slowly and use up to 2 hours easily. If you must go fast, speed up in Step 8 through Step 12. But leave at least 40 minutes for Step 13 and Step 14. These steps are most important since they bring home the message.

4. When you debrief, keep your role as discussion facilitator and paraphraser. Try not to "preach" to the group. Patience will pay off. Read through the following full section to alert yourself to the messages which generally come out during the discussion. Do not try to force out more than the group is willing to initiate, because the forced points probably will not be meaningful anyway. Keep the extra points in mind, note them, and use some other activities in this book to help bring them to your faculty.

5. Note that in Step 13 there are many sample questions. You will no doubt not need to ask every question, since many of the points will come to the floor without your solicitation. Ask only those questions you want to ask and need to ask in order to keep the discussion going.

6. If you are a principal, for example, and do not feel comfortable in leading this simulation game with your faculty, then by all means ask someone else to lead it. A vice-principal, a guidance counselor, or a central office curriculum coordinator is an excellent person to be the leader. You can be a participant or observer, as you see fit.

WHY USE THIS SIMULATION GAME: QUOTATIONS AND COMMENTARY REGARDING THE MESSAGE

Because it is sometimes difficult to read through a simulation game and project the actions as well as the remarks of the players, let us present some of our experiences in utilizing "The Cousin's Choice: Fake or Real." Here are 5 quotes that are illustrative and powerful.

Teacher: This is the first faculty meeting that I can recall that we talked about something really important to us all.

Teacher: I knew in my head—well, you know, I knew it intellectually—but now I feel it in the gut what it means to be double-crossed. After Bill zapped me by going real when I went fake, I wanted revenge. That's all I felt. Now I know how the kids feel when they are promised one thing but get another.

Supervisor: This whole game came home to me when I realized that my partner and I changed our decisions after Round 10. From Round 11 to 20 we had it made together. When we were back to back, nothing. When we were face to face, we planned together and it worked out O.K. Just a few minutes of face to face communication meant a whole lot.

Teacher: We developed a sense of trust when we talked together. Before we talked we didn't trust each other.

Supervisor: This is just like supervising. When I trust the teacher and he trusts me, we're in good shape. But if I try to get him, then he tries to get me back and vice versa. And that's not good.

These quotes are just a few examples. Let us now spell out explicitly 8 messages that this simulation game has the potential to bring out to the faculty. This simple and effective simulation will lead the group to make some of—if not all or more than—the following points, which are all part of improving supervision.

1. *Face to face communication is desirable between people.* Even a few minutes of direct personal talking can change the subsequent behavior of people who have not been talking to each other. (Note during the debriefing how many people comment on the effect of the short communication period between the 10th and 11th decisions.)

2. *When people have a common problem to solve, they will think together and plan together.* The common problem of all teachers and supervisors is the improvement of the tone of the school in general, as well as the specific improvement of classroom teaching. Whether the players are teachers, supervisors, or a mixed group, there is a common school problem for them which they will work on together.

3. *People can, and generally do, develop mutual trust when they solve a problem together and talk it through.* People do not generally start off with much mutual trust before they can communicate meaningfully with each other. Mutual trust takes time and effort to develop. Each person must see that it is to his advantages to develop a trusting relationship.

4. *Different people have different interpretations of the same directive.* The directive given in Step 5, "do the best you can," means different things to the players. Some try to compete with their partner to see who can gain more money. Some try to cooperate with their partner. Though each person heard the same words, there were different interpretations due to the different frames of reference the players had.

5. *Different motivations and reasons may be behind common decisions.* Some players decide for Real because of moral reasons. They simply refuse to lie and say they are someone else. Their commitment to honesty is great, and it leads them to tell the truth at all times. Some players decide for Real because they are cautious. They do not want to risk losing the minimum $50,000 they can gain by staying with a real decision. Some players decide for Real because they fear the possible penalty from the court if they are caught as a "fake" nephew. Some people decide for Real because, as a "fake" nephew, they would have to leave their current life and start another one in a faraway place.

   Some people decide for Fake because of the potential high gain of money. Their desire for money leads them to be a "fake" nephew. Some people decide for Fake because this offers them the possibility of starting life anew in a faraway place. Some people decide for Fake because they enjoy taking risks and want to see what happens when they do so.

6. *If a person breaks an agreement with another person, or violates an established feeling of mutual trust, the hurt person feels angry and often seeks revenge.* When a player is "zapped" by his partner, he tries to get even in the next few decisions, or even by misleading him during the 3–5 minute communication period. If a person is zapped on the 20th decision and there is now no way to get even, then he remains quite angry.

7. *When people understand themselves and know the consequences of their behavior, then they have an excellent opportunity to change their behavior.* Feedback from someone else helps them to decide in a more knowledgeable way. (Note that when the players find out, after the 10th decision, what their partner thinks and feels about their decisions, then they can negotiate and plan their future decisions with added understanding. When they see the results of their behavior and reason them through with their partner, then they often change their direction. Many people alter their course after only 3–5 minutes of directly seeing the consequences of their first 10 decisions.)

8. *When people are emotionally charged up, they often do not act in a logical, reasonable way.* Our emotional state does affect the way we think. (Note that when some player feels angry and revengeful, he may give up acting reasonably just to get even with his partner. He may make decisions he previously rejected just to get back at his partner.)

Perhaps not all of the above 8 messages will come out on the floor in any one given debriefing discussion. Surely three or four will be voiced by the faculty. But even these three or four make this simulation game, "The Cousin's Choice: Fake or Real," worthwhile for the faculty.

APPLICATION

The leader of this simulation game has the potential of leading his faculty to apply the messages voiced by the group. If you are playing with teachers, then you can direct the discussion and application to classroom teaching as well as general school affairs. If you are playing with other supervisors, then you can direct the discussion to the supervision process as well as general school affairs. If the players are a mixed group of teachers and supervisors, then the focus can be on either teaching or supervision.

If you have time after the entire simulation game is over, you can immediately launch into an application session. Since there usually is not much more time available, you should plan for an application session soon afterwards.

The application session should begin with a few excerpts from the debriefing discussion, with identification of the people who made these interesting remarks. Then there should be a listing of some of the important points made by the faculty. This is best done by writing out and distributing a sheet to the faculty. This procedure will refresh everyone's memory, give the faculty something to focus on, and give you an opportunity to select those messages you particularly want your faculty to attend to. A sample summary sheet follows—one is the blank form (Figure 11-5) and one is a sample one completed as a guide (Figure 11-6). Look it over carefully to note this principal point of view.

The application session should aim to push forward. If several sub-groups seem particularly interested in different key messages, then the leader can break the faculty up into small task groups. If the decision is to focus on only one key issue, then the

TO: _____

FROM: _____

RE: Follow-up from the Simulation Game, "The Cousin's Choice: Fake or Real," led by _____ on _____, 19_____.

1. *Quotable quotes from the session:*

   A.

   B.

   C.

2. *Key points raised:*

   A.

   B

   C

3. *Decisions to follow through for implementation:*

Figure 11-5
Simulation Game Summary Sheet—Blank Form

TO: _Faculty_

FROM: _Pat Robinson, Principal_

RE: Follow-up from the Simulation Game, "The Cousin's Choice: Fake or Real," led by _Ruth Romano_ on _4/26/_ , 19____ .

1. *Quotable quotes from the session:*

   A. _Sarah Keers, "Well I'll be darned. I never knew how much I trusted Don before."_

   B. _Elaine Pollack, "When you give trust you can get it back. When you don't, you don't get trusted. I gave so I was trusted._

   C. _John Weiss, "Let's face it. Now everyone knows for sure that I am the real John Weiss. I am for real."_

2. *Key points raised:*

   A. _A trusting teacher develops trusting students._

   B. _Open communication channels facilitate better understanding among people- faculty to faculty; faculty to student._

   C. _"Real" people win out in the end._

3. *Decisions to follow through for implementation:*

   This is the agenda for our next meeting. Let's spend some time deciding how to create trust and open channels.

Figure 11-6
Simulation Game Summary Sheet—Completed Form
201

group can proceed as a whole or break up into small groups. In any case, the leader should direct the faculty to work on specific changes in what they do.

    A. Direct them to be specific.
    B. Request some "Do's"—positive things to do. *Emphasize this part strongly.*
    C. Request (but do not emphasize) some "Don'ts"—negative things to eliminate.

Case Example #1 - High School

As a way to implement face-to-face communication, our sub-group recommends that:

    1. We institute two evening programs per semester where the faculty and selected club leaders discuss school problems. For example, we might see the film *No Reason to Stay* and then talk about it together.
    2. Each teacher hold a conference day once each month where students can raise problems that are on their mind. The conference day should be chaired by the homeroom. Perhaps we might even play this game about the "Cousins" with our students.

Case Example #2 - District Curriculum Coordinators of Subject Area Specialties

    1. We plan to work on better communication with the teachers by regular scheduled visits, by reducing our written communications, and increasing personal chats at the faculty room. We'll meet them more than halfway. We'll meet them at their schools at their departmental meetings.

If you want to try more than the usual type of application session, try BRAIN-STORMING to get new, fresh ideas. See Chapter 12 for suggestions on "How to Utilize Brainstorming with Your Faculty."

CONCLUDING WORDS

A supervisor can use this simulation game directly with his faculty or with his fellow supervisors. In either case, this particular simulation game will help in supervision because its messages apply to teachers and supervisors, all of whom are interested in the improvement of teaching. The messages of "The Cousin's Choice: Fake or Real" are important and the simulation game format brings them out with meaning and strength.

Chapter 12

How to Utilize Brainstorming With Your Faculty

How To Utilize Brainstorming With Your Faculty

INTRODUCTION AND OBJECTIVES

Brainstorming is a strategy often talked about and admired, but too little used. It comes to us from group dynamics experts, who have sought ways of finding new, fresh answers to perplexing problems. Surely, supervisors have many continuing problems that need and deserve a fresh look, too. Thus, with the complexity of school life and teacher-supervisor relations today, the strategy of brainstorming merits an opportunity to show us how it can help in supervision.

This chapter will devote itself to presenting a procedure for utilizing brainstorming with your faculty and some examples of its use.

At the conclusion of this chapter, the reader should be able to:

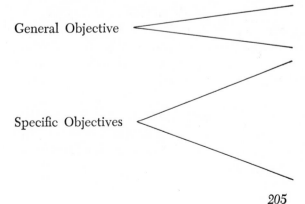

General Objective

1. Understand what brainstorming is and how it can be a helpful strategy in a supervision program.

Specific Objectives

2. List at least 5 reasons why brainstorming succeeds with teachers.

3. Conduct a brainstorming session by following the step-by-step procedure.

4. Give an account of a brainstorming session by referring to events and follow-up quotations.

WHY USE BRAINSTORMING WITH YOUR FACULTY

The basic reason for using the brainstorming strategy with your faculty is most simple —it works. Brainstorming is an effective strategy for solving problems and reducing rough spots in specific school areas. This strategy works because the developer sought and refined the steps which lead to positive results.

Specifically, brainstorming succeeds because it has many characteristics consistent with what research tells us is a good learning situation.

First, brainstorming gets everyone involved in the problem solving task. Each person, as you will see soon from the procedural steps offered later, participates in the brainstorming activity.

Second, because each person is actively participating, people are stimulated and enthusiastic. The brainstorming pace is lively, and it is therefore impossible to mentally fall asleep. On the contrary, participants are involved and eager.

Third, teachers find brainstorming attractive because it motivates them through acceptance by the leader (the supervisor) and the other participants (the teachers). When a teacher contributes an idea, neither the leader nor another participant criticizes him. Everybody, as stated by the rules of brainstorming, accepts the teacher's contribution. This acceptance without criticism is, in effect, positive reinforcement which, in turn, motivates the teacher to continue offering more ideas. The absence of a put-down leads the teacher to step up.

Fourth, brainstorming helps the teachers focus on their problem solving task by offering an organized procedure to follow. There is neither time nor incentive to stray from the issue at hand. Hence, brainstorming is productive, since each participant is contributing to and helping in the common group effort.

Fifth, this procedure, in which everyone contributes to a common group task, conveys a distinct non-verbal message: we can work together to solve a common problem. This message creates the basis for an improved environment to work. It also lays the foundation for better personal relationships among the supervisor and the teachers. People realize that if they can work together on solving a common problem, then they probably can work together in harmony on other tasks as well, provided they each respect the other's contribution.

Sixth, especially for those people who have done little or no brainstorming, this strategy offers a welcomed creative approach to problem solving. Brainstorming promotes creativity and spontaneity in thought and, hence, teachers respond well.

Seventh, teachers are willing to follow through with their ideas because they themselves have created the ideas. As in other areas and other people, teachers are willing to pursue ideas, suggestions, and programs to a significant degree when they have generated the idea themselves. This is natural because the teachers have a real stake in the matter.

Eighth, brainstorming offers variety simply because it is not used as frequently as other strategies. Faculties which use the same strategies all of the time tend to become sluggish. The variety offered by brainstorming serves to spur on a faculty, and it adds a pinch of spice to enliven creative thought.

In short, brainstorming is a strategy for creatively working with your faculty in solving some problems or resolving some conflicts. It is an easily used strategy that is effective in terms of the solutions reached and the general climate established within the faculty.

Let us now turn to an example of using brainstorming. We shall follow it with the effective step-by-step strategy for brainstorming.

AN EXAMPLE OF USING BRAINSTORMING: A CASE STUDY

We have used the brainstorming strategy to tackle many problems, including "how to improve faculty meetings" and "how to improve our teacher supervision process." The most dramatic one of all, however, was with a problem concerning report cards in a local high school.

The teachers of Kennedy High School and the Board of Education came to an impasse over the reporting system to be used beginning September, 1973. Communication between the teachers and the members of the board was less than satisfactory and mostly in angry tones. During a meeting in which we simply explored the history of the problem as a way for each person to ventilate his dissatisfaction with the situation, we agreed to convene a week later to brainstorm in order to resolve the existing conflict. We agreed to invite board members, incumbent and incoming student council officers, and a teacher representative from each department of the school. We agreed that we would try to come up with an acceptable solution to be submitted to the total faculty, total Board of Education, superintendent, and high school principal.

At the next meeting, we had 16 people: 3 students, 3 members of the Board of Education, and 10 teachers. We divided into 2 small groups to keep it real cozy and make it easy for the students and board members to talk with the teachers. We prepared a ditto sheet of the rules (see Step 3 later in this chapter) and distributed it to each person. We went over the rules orally, and then each group selected its own recorder. We briefly identified the problem again, so that it was clear to everyone present. The present report cards were unacceptable to the teachers, yet no new method had been successfully worked out.

Below is a list of *main* points following each of the main questions as put together by the two groups.

A. What's wrong with our report card?

There are two systems, not one, on the card now.

Responsibility is totally the teacher's.
Gradations for a passing level, but none for failure.

The 0.5 average means you goof off late in the term, and still pass if you did well early in the semester.

Final exams don't really count.
Student can withdraw if he sees he's failing.

B. What can we do specifically to improve our report card?
   Remove the 0.5 average for passing.
   Use a unified, single system for the report cards.
   Let final exams count up to $\frac{1}{5}$ of grade.
   Give an arithmetic range to letter grades

   $A = 93–100\%$
   $B = 86–92\%$
   $C = 77–85\%$
   $D = 70–76\%$
   $E = 0–69\%$

   Average the grades so as to reflect all 4 quarters' grades.

   Announce at beginning of term what will constitute each letter grade.

   Give a separate grade for effort—different from achievement.

C. What will prevent us from implementing these improvements for our report cards?

   Disapproval by the rest of the teachers.
   Disapproval by the Board of Education.
   Lack of an integrated scheme for these suggestions.
   Our inability to convince the others who are not present.
   Anticipation of the new curriculum change in 2 years.

At this point, each of the two groups rank ordered its own list. Then, the recorders alternately read off each item and the total group discussed the positive and negative features of each one. Some items were "withdrawn" from the list by consensus.

D. What next steps should we take?
   A short powwow to make a package proposal.
   Combine the positive suggestions into one comprehensive one.
   Each one of us then talk up support for our proposal.

Since there was a great desire for a combined, acceptable proposal now by the whole group, we recessed for ten minutes to gather our spirits and thoughts. Several people caucused over coffee with paper and pencil in hand. When we re-convened, they read their combined proposal, which incorporated the positive points listed above. Within 20 minutes all rough spots were ironed out, and a proposal was accepted by the group.

At this point, we delegated one person to write up a full draft proposal to be circulated to all present for approval. We summarized the key aspects and accomplishments of the brainstorming session, so that we all would be aware of what happened. Then we broke up.

The draft proposal was prepared within 3 days. It was approved by those at the brainstorming session, and later approved overwhelmingly by the entire faculty of the high school. At the next meeting of the Board of Education, the board members approved the proposal, relying heavily on the report of those members who had brainstormed.

A significant by-product of the entire endeavor was the creation of a positive climate among the teachers, the students, and the parents (board members). Communication channels opened up again and people began to talk freely with each other again. An air of optimism arose, which replaced the pessimism and distrust that was so evident earlier. In short, it was an amazing turnaround after only one brief meeting and a brainstorming session.

A STEP-BY-STEP STRATEGY FOR BRAINSTORMING

Though brainstorming is a creative and lively experience within an informal atmosphere, it is necessary for you as the leader to carefully plan and conduct the session. You will need to choose a topic that involves alternative solutions, rather than a topic with just a choice between only two possibilities. The care and strategy you use with this topic will then enhance the effectiveness of the brainstorming effort. Below are some steps which we have found helpful. After you have followed them once or twice, feel free to creatively modify them to suit your own style.

Step 1. Divide your faculty into small groups, so that each group has between 6–12 people. Too small or too large a group will impede communication and spontaneity within each small group of teachers. If you do not have a large faculty, you might even wish to keep everyone in one group of 25–30 teachers. Be careful, however, that the group is not so large that some people will withdraw and not participate actively.

Step 2. Seat the small groups around tables or in small circles. If you have one group that is large, seat the teachers in a semicircle facing you. This will facilitate communication.

Step 3. Announce that the group will be brainstorming on a current problem of interest—that is, "We're going to storm our brains together for a solution." Point out that there will be certain ground rules which everyone must follow. You may read, post, or distribute the rules below:

   a. Suggest any idea that occurs to you—even what might seem like a "far out" or "wild" idea, since any suggestion may trigger other ideas for someone else. Be a freewheeler.

   b. Focus only on the specific problem at hand and nothing else.

   c. Feel free to build on, "piggyback," or "hitchhike" on ideas of other people. Feel free to add on to other ideas or to combine other ideas for an idea of your own.

    d. Suggest as many ideas as you can; quantity counts.

    e. DO NOT criticize or say anything negative about any ideas offered in the beginning. (There will be time later for analysis.) No "put-downs" of any kind are allowed.

Repeat these rules and emphasize their importance.

Step 4. Select a reporter for each small group and supply him with pencil and paper. If you keep your faculty in one group, then you can use the chalkboard to record ideas. Be sure there is lots of board space. Even better than the chalkboard are large sheets of easel paper and a felt-tip marker so that you can have a tangible record available later on, as well as a visible growing list of ideas to serve as ongoing motivation.

Step 5. Announce the topic for brainstorming. Tell what the *specific* problem is so that each person will be clear about the sought-after solution. For example, you might announce that the group will brainstorm on report cards and indicate the obvious dissatisfaction of the faculty with the current report card, as evidenced in the last faculty meeting. In choosing the problem for brainstorming, be sure to select one that has *alternative solutions rather than one with an either-or solution,* since the latter does not lend itself to brainstorming.

Step 6. Ask the teachers to begin according to the rules given above by addressing themselves to the question. They might ask, for example: "What's wrong with our report cards?" By starting with a list of negatives, the teachers will alert themselves to the specific negative features in the topic and also warm themselves up for suggestion solutions. Recorders in small groups should record every idea offered. Either you as leader, or a separate recorder, should record ideas on the large sheets of paper, if you keep the faculty in one group.

Step 7. After a reasonable time, or when the group runs dry, ask the group to begin on Phase 2. Here, for example, the teachers address themselves to the question: "What can we do specifically to improve our report cards?" This is the crux of the brainstorming session, so emphasize and repeat the rules concerning freewheeling, quantity, and no criticism. Ask everyone to help you enforce the rules and remind recorders to record each suggestion.

Step 8. Begin this step when the group is finished spouting ideas. If you have more than one group, ask each group to quickly choose 1–4 ideas it wishes to briefly share with the other groups. The group recorder can communicate the selected items after a minute or two.

Step 9. Ask the teachers now to address themselves to the question, "What will prevent us from implementing these improvements for our report cards?" Here, the teacher should keep in mind their responses to the first two questions in Steps 6 and 7. They can also consider what they have heard from any other group, too.

Step 10. When they have completed their responses, ask them to look over all the responses they have made so far. Now ask them to rank order the suggested improvements from Step 7 from most to least preferred. If they cannot rank order all the items, then they should pick at least the top 5 in rank order.

Step 11. Here is the opportunity to present the positive and negative aspects of the responses. Ask each group recorder to begin at the top of this rank order list for his group and request (a) strengths and advantages, and then (b) weaknesses and disadvantages from the members for each item. Inter-personal conversation is permitted at this time. Teachers should make their comments in light of the responses given to the 3 questions asked so far in Steps 6, 7, and 9.

Step 12. If you have more than one group, then ask each group recorder to briefly report to the other groups at this time.

Step 13. Ask the teachers to respond now to the final question in light of all that has gone previously. Teachers should address themselves to the question by asking, for example: "What steps should we take next?" Teachers should suggest ways to move to action.

Step 14. At this point, you will need to summarize and bring the brainstorming session to an end. If you have several groups, ask each group recorder to briefly report the responses he has. Then you can tie it all together with a few summary comments. If you have kept the faculty as a single group, briefly review the responses in the various steps as a summary.

Step 15. Once the teachers have finished, they will be keyed up and yet pleased that the brainstorming session is finished. Either now as part of the summary or very soon afterwards, you must "take the next step." You must decide what to do beyond just brainstorming. You obviously have several options. You can prepare a written report of the session and distribute it to everyone vitally concerned. (Here is where the recorder's sheet and/or the large easel sheets are helpful.) Or you can organize a committee to take the initial steps suggested by the teachers. For example, a group of teachers could begin redesigning the report card so as to incorporate the suggestions made for improvement. Or, you can pick one of the suggested next steps from Step 12 and initiate it. Whatever you choose will be your judgment, but you need to move beyond the brainstorming session.

QUOTATIONS FROM BRAINSTORMERS

I'm pooped!

I never thought so hard and so fast before!

I particularly like the idea that we identified things that would prevent us from succeeding. Then I realized—and I think the others did too—that really nothing much was holding us back. So we flew.

It's nice to know that I can think again.

Time passed so fast; I was fully involved.

Great—and we solved it besides.

Well, we did beat the clock, didn't we?

I feel so good. What's that saying, "This is the calm after the storm." Well, I'm calm now that I've been stormed.

Chapter 13

How to Help Teachers Write Performance Objectives

13

How To Help Teachers Write
Performance Objectives

INTRODUCTION AND OBJECTIVES

One of the more recent trends in American education has been the turn to performance objectives for teachers. This goes along with the trend in curriculum development to list objectives for texts, units, and lessons. These trends began gaining momentum in the early 1960's. By the early 1970's, they had gained acceptance in many quarters, while still being challenged in others. Some supervisors may decide that teacher performance objectives at this time are not appropriate for their teachers. If so, then they should use this chapter for acquainting just themselves with performance objectives. Indeed, there are times and situations in which a supervisor may, correctly, not initiate the use and writing of performance objectives. Yes, the disagreement between the "pro-objectives" and the "anti-objectives" sides is unresolved, and an absolutist position is unwarranted for all schools at this time.

With this cautionary acknowledgement in mind, this chapter will focus on the writing of performance objectives for teachers by offering guidelines, a training strategy, and suggestions for following up the training session.

At the conclusion of this chapter, the reader should be able to:

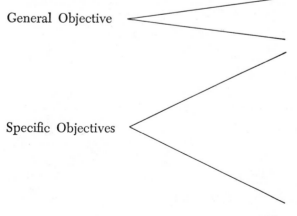

General Objective

1. Understand the value of teacher performance objectives and how to help teachers write them.

Specific Objectives

2. List at least 4 advantages for using teacher performance objectives.

3. Conduct a training session for writing teacher performance objectives by following the step-by-step strategy presented.

4. Know how to follow up the training session by utilizing some of the suggestions offered.

215

THE ROLE AND VALUE OF TEACHER PERFORMANCE OBJECTIVES

Teacher performance objectives offer the supervisor and teacher an excellent opportunity to think through just what they want to accomplish during the school year. The supervisor and the teacher can sit down and work out in writing, for future reference, what the teacher should focus on as he seeks to perform his job effectively. Teacher performance objectives have the following values:

1. They require the teacher and supervisor to explicitly focus their intentions in relation to the entire school context.

2. They require the teacher and supervisor to convene an initial meeting to know each other better.

3. They require the teacher and supervisor to set down in writing their expectations, so as to have guidelines for future conferences, observations, and evaluations.

4. They require the teacher and supervisor to make decisions which they might otherwise delay for too long.

5. They provide the teacher and supervisor with the opportunity to tie together the various elements of the teacher's task in the school.

6. They offer an opportunity to talk about improvement of teaching rather than only maintenance of the status quo.

7. They set the context for future planning in curiculum and teaching.

It is important to mention, here at the outset, that the value of teacher performance objectives increases when both teacher and supervisor are flexible. Conditions in school change from September through June. Therefore, the flexible teacher and supervisor will wisely confer regularly, to reassess the general situation and decide whether there is a need for new teacher performance objectives. Perhaps some objectives will deserve to be neglected in light of new ones. If the teacher and supervisor are not flexible, they will pass up good opportunities to update and improve themselves. They might well pass up the opportunity to set forth new objectives, which may be of even greater value than the original ones. After all, it is certainly impossible to foresee and predetermine all worthwhile objectives. On the other hand, flexibility does not imply the ready and easy opportunity to get rid of old objectives not yet accomplished.

SETTING THE STAGE FOR WRITING TEACHER PERFORMANCE OBJECTIVES

a. Establishing a Climate for a Training Session

Obviously, it is essential that there be a facilitating atmosphere before teachers are requested to write their performance objectives. The overall context must be supportive, or efforts to have the teachers write will lead to eruptions of anger and distrust. Many teachers are threatened by requests for them to write teacher performance objectives. Unless they feel comfortable that the entire endeavor is worthwhile and mutually beneficial, they will resist strongly. Indeed, with some united effort based on open hostility, teachers can easily sabotage a supervisor's plan.

It is not necessary here to launch into a long section on the need for you to establish a trusting relationship with your teachers. Nor is it necessary to even reiterate all the many details you will need to attend to in order to establish this atmosphere. Suffice it to say that you need to carefully gain the support of your supervisory colleagues and the Board of Education, if necessary. Through a series of faculty meetings and reports, you must establish the purpose and sincerity of your request for writing teacher performance. Teachers will need to sense your seriousness, sincerity, and confidence over some time before they will go along with you. In short, you need their cooperation, or else the efforts to write objectives will backfire. General practice for gaining a cooperative spirit in the faculty applies here, and you should use it strategically.

Once you feel that a supportive climate exists for the writing of objectives, then you can plan and hold a workshop or training session to teach your teachers standard, acceptable procedures. A workshop structure provides an informal, non-threatening setting which can further your efforts and reinforce the positive atmosphere. Therefore, choose a comfortable room for the workshop which will facilitate discussion among your teachers similar to the one used for brainstorming (see the chapter devoted to brainstorming).

Before beginning the training session, you should carefully read the next few pages, since they form the basis of the workshop. In addition, you will be distributing these sheets to your teachers towards the end of the workshop as a summarizing technique. These sheets give guidelines and strategies for writing performance objectives.

GUIDELINES FOR WRITING TEACHER PERFORMANCE OBJECTIVES

Guideline #1. Describe the expected *behavior* of the *teacher*.

Guideline #2. Describe an *observable behavior* in terms of an outcome verb the teacher will perform (e.g., write, identify, attend meetings, chair a committee).

Guideline #3. Describe *important conditions* which identify the time, environment, resources, restraints, or limitations under which the teacher will perform the behavior. (Completion time is assumed to be the school year unless otherwise specified.)

Guideline #4. Describe *standards* for an acceptable performance.

Guideline #5. State only *one outcome verb* in each objective.

Guideline #6. *Avoid and/or minimize* objectives that involve *joint performance* by two or more teachers.

Guideline #7. *Subsume* sets of *specific* performance objectives under an appropriate, more *general* objective. The specific items listed should be important and representative *indicators* of the general heading.

Keep them realistic and attainable, yet challenging.

STRATEGY FOR WRITING TEACHER PERFORMANCE OBJECTIVES: AFFECTIVE AND NON-VERBAL QUALITIES

1. Select and state the affective or non-verbal quality yourself.

2. Identify a classroom (or person) which possesses this quality.

3. Observe the classroom (or person).

4. List behaviors which indicate this quality.

5. Identify a classroom (or person) which does not possess this quality.

6. Observe the classroom (or person).

7. List some behaviors which do not indicate this quality.

8. Select from the two lists appropriate behaviors to aim for.

9. Write affective and non-verbal objectives based on these indicators. Check and follow the Guidelines for Writing Teacher Performance Objectives.

10. Mutually agree upon objectives—teachers and supervisors should mutually agree to a set of objectives.

STRATEGY FOR WRITING TEACHER PERFORMANCE OBJECTIVES: PEDAGOGICAL AND COGNITIVE

1. Select and state the general objective yourself.

2. Place under each general objective some (1–3) specific objectives, or specific behavioral phrases.

3. Describe a standard for an acceptable performance.

4. Check to see that specific objectives or phrases are representative indicators of the general objective.

5. Seek help in selecting and writing objectives when it is difficult to state the general objective, indicate the specifics appropriate for a general objective, or state a standard for acceptance. Check and follow the Guidelines for Writing Teacher Performance Objectives.

6. Discuss objectives (that is, revise and refine objectives with help of colleagues, including teachers and supervisors).

7. Mutually agree upon objectives—teachers and supervisors should mutually agree to a set of objectives.

TRAINING SESSION FOR WRITING PERFORMANCE OBJECTIVES

Let us turn to the training session specifically and relate teacher performance objectives to classroom teaching. (See Chapters, 4, 5, 6, and 7 dealing with Classroom Climate, Pedagogical Interaction Patterns, Cognitive Processes, and Use of Space and Student Groupings.)

A STEP-BY-STEP TRAINING SESSION FOR WRITING TEACHER PERFORMANCE OBJECTIVES

Step 1. Distribute the sheet "Classroom Qualities" (Figure 13-1) and ask your teachers to fill it out. This exercise concerns mainly the affective and non-verbal domain and is an effective way to get teachers to discuss the affective aspect of their performance.

Step 2. By a quick show of hands, find out which item is the top ranked one. That is, which one appears to be rank 1 for the group. Probably, this will be the item with the single most votes for rank 1.

Step 3. Briefly discuss this item and other items of particular concern.

Step 4. Ask each teacher to list 3 indicators of this rank 1 quality. That is, what behavior or activities, in *your* classroom, indicate the presence of the quality.

Step 5. Ask each teacher, on his own, to take his own top 2 qualities other than the one already done, and to list 3 indicators for these 2 qualities.

Step 6. Request teachers to share their indicators with each other.

Step 7. Ask teachers to identify behavior or activities in their classroom or another classroom which indicates the lack or slighting of these qualities.

Name _____   *Date* _____

Classroom Qualities

Here are 10 qualities that you might find in a classroom. Place a 1 next to the item you think is most important in your classroom, a 2 next to the second most important item, and so forth. The items appear in alphabetical order.

A. _____ Creativity
B. _____ Equality
C. _____ Fairness
D. _____ Intellectual spirit
E. _____ Interaction between students
F. _____ Orderliness
G. _____ Patience
H. _____ Purposefulness
I. _____ Quiet
J. _____ Respect

Figure 13-1
Classroom Qualities Checklist

Step 8. Ask each teacher to choose one of these 3 qualities, based on the positive and negative indicators, for writing his first performance objective.

Step 9. At this point distribute the examples called "Affective and Non-verbal Classroom Examples." (Figure 13-2) Go over the examples with the teacher. Keep in mind that these are examples based on the "Guidelines for Writing Teacher Performance Objectives" listed previously. A key point may concern the standard for an acceptable performance. That is, how can we measure the presence of the quality. Keep in mind that these items on the Classroom Qualities Sheet (Figure 13-1) relate closely to the observational instruments presented earlier in this book in Chapters 4, 5, 6 and 7 dealing with Classroom Climate, Pedagogical Interaction Patterns, Cognitive Processes, and Use of Space and Student Groupings. If you have used these instruments with your faculty, you can remind the teachers of them and the relationship. If not, simply point out the existence of the instruments which you can later explore with them. In either case, it is wise to acknowledge the difficulty in measuring and establishing a standard for acceptance. Yet point out that some kind of standard is necessary, that at this time there is no great need for 100% precision, that teachers should just list what seems reasonable now, and that in the long run, supervisors and teachers will discuss this at length. Try not to get bogged down here.

Step 10. Ask the teachers individually, in pairs, or in trios to write a performance objective. Ask them to do the best they can here now.

Step 11. Briefly share the written objective among the teachers. Request some suggestions for improvement and comments about the shared objectives.

Step 12. Ask the teachers to write one or two more similar objectives in light of the comments just made.

Step 13. Briefly share these objectives, too, requesting comments as you go along.

Step 14. After you have shared the written objectives, point out that there is yet another type of performance objectives closely related to the one the group has been working on. This type concerns the Pedagogical and Cognitive dimensions of teacher behavior. This is best clarified by simply looking at the set of terms associated with this type. Distribute the sheet entitled "Some General Terms in Teacher Performance" (Figure 13-3), which follows.

Step 15. Ask the teachers to select any one of the seven terms to work on.

Step 16. Ask teachers to write 2–4 specific terms as indicators of the general terms they have chosen. That is to say, if they have chosen the term Learn More About (#2), then they should write 2–4 specific terms which show in what way a teacher might "learn more about" his

AFFECTIVE AND NON-VERBAL CLASSROOM EXAMPLES

1. This year I will show greater respect of the pupils in my classroom by my ability to
   a. talk with them "heart to heart"
   b. drastically reduce the sarcasm I use
   c. attract more after school pupil visitors.
   This objective can be evaluated through a student questionnaire or interviews; ask the kids themselves.

2. This year I, Joan Bailey, will strive to add creativeness to my classroom lessons as demonstrated by my
   a. using the fine arts in Social Studies and English activities along with my students
   b. encouraging individualized special projects where students will be creative
   The standard of acceptance will be an increase of 4–5 points in Creativity on Tuckman's scale over my score in May, 1973.

3. Tom Gaynor will have a less quiet (that is, more active) classroom next year starting September. This will be demonstrated by his
   a. having more small group projects simultaneously
   b. having a scattered seat arrangement around the room to force students and him to move around in order to communicate
   c. having students participate more in discussion
      This can be judged by observing with the same instrument used this year to measure student talk. The standard of acceptance is: 10% better than this year.

4. I will *be* a more *creative* teacher in the classroom this coming year in the discussions I lead, lessons I plan, and the units I teach, as shown by my ability to
   a. come up with many ideas I've not tried so far in 5 years
   b. integrate art and music activities with language arts so students will participate more
   c. schedule student interest hours at least twice weekly
   d. employ the ideas I learn at the U. of Buffalo's creativity institute this summer
   You can evaluate this calmly with me anyway you decide that is reasonable.

5. This year, I (teacher John Sherman) will become a fairer teacher in class discussions and in use of materials as demonstrated by my ability to
   a. select non-sexist reading matter
   b. choose girls and boys equally often in a discussion
   c. check homework anonymously
   d. grade classwork and tests anonymously
   Objective may be measured by checking my lesson plans for selected material and observing my class discussions. Success will be 15% better (fairer) than last year.

Figure 13-2
Affective and Non-Verbal Affective Examples

Some General Terms in Teacher Performance

1. Understand
2. Learn more about
3. Develop an interest
4. Appreciate
5. Become familiar with
6. Clarify
7. Know

Figure 13-3
General Terms In Teacher Performance

students, for example. A teacher might learn more about his students by *identifying their interests* and *recognizing their mutual preferences*

Step 17. At this point, distribute the "Pedagogical and Cognitive Classroom Examples, shown in Figure 13-4". Go over the examples with the teachers. Once again, keep in mind that these are examples based on the "Guidelines for Writing Teacher Performance Objectives."

Step 18. Ask the teachers individually, in pairs, or in trios to write a performance objective based on the general and specific terms. Ask them to do the best they can here now.

Step 19. Briefly share the written objectives among the teachers. Request some suggestions for improvement and comments about the shared objectives.

Step 20. Ask the teachers to write one or two more similar objectives in light of the comments just made.

Step 21. Briefly share these objectives, too, requesting comments as you go along.

Step 22. Summarize here. You can easily and effectively do this by distributing the following three sheets: (1) Guidelines for Writing Teacher Performance Objectives, (2) Strategy for Writing Teacher Performance Objectives: Affective and Non-verbal Qualities, and (3) Strategy for writing Teacher Performance Objectives: Pedagogical and Cognitive. These sheets indicate what the teachers have essentially done so far.

Step 23. Point out, in addition, that teachers can and should write teacher performance objectives related to aspects of their jobs and lives other than their classroom teaching. For example, the teachers can write objectives related to their positions as members of a school faculty (see Chapter 2 on Institutional Activities) or related to their personal development. If you wish, you may want to take some time to write one or two of

PEDAGOGICAL AND COGNITIVE CLASSROOM EXAMPLES

1. I will shift my teaching style when I conduct group discussions this year, as shown by
   a. getting students to ask more questions of each other
   b. asking fewer questions for fact answers
   c. asking more questions to which I don't have a "correct" answer, like: "Should we abolish the income tax?"
   This objective can be measured by observing my classes and scoring it with the Pedagogical Moves Instrument and the Verification Instrument.

2. I will work with my student on learning how to deal with value issues this year, as demonstrated in
   a. conducting more value clarification lessons
   b. asking more value questions on personal feelings
   This can be assessed by comparing it with last year according to supervisory records. Success will be a 7–10% improvement.

3. Stanley West will improve his understanding of earth science this year as shown by
   a. attending a graduate seminar once a week for credit and passing it
   b. reading at least 3 new books on science

   This objective will be measured by my success in the seminar class and my oral presentation to the faculty at one in-service day workshop.

4. This term, I (teacher John Sherman) will learn more about my slow readers through observation in free activity, individualized study periods, and group activities, as demonstrated by my ability to
   a. identify their interests in reading.
   b. determine the classmates who can help them improve and will help them.
   c. recognize mutual preferences in reading.
   d. identify their particular problem points in reading.
   Objective may be measured by my log of activities, a self-evaluation regarding improved attention to my slow readers, and observational comments by my reading supervisor.

5. Linda Morgan will devote more time to thinking and student talking next year in conducting classroom discussions, as shown by my being able to
   a. achieve long wait-time after a student talks
   b. achieve long wait-time after I talk
   c. not interrupt during a student's answer or remarks
   Measurement of this will be through observation and recording of actual classroom events. Just watch and decide.

Figure 13-4
Pedagogical and Cognitive Classroom Examples

these now. The emphasis here has been on teacher performance objectives related to classroom teaching, so as to relate closely with previous chapters on observation. See Chapters 4, 5, 6, and 7 dealing with Classroom Climate, Pedagogical Interaction Patterns, Cognitive Processes, and Use of Space and Student Groupings.

Step 24. Close the training workshop by setting up a schedule with the teachers about future practice sessions and/or submission of their own actual performance objectives for conference purposes.

FOLLOWING-THROUGH AFTER THE TRAINING WORKSHOP

It is essential that you follow up the training session with further encouragement, help, and conferring. You will generate enthusiasm and skill via the training workshop. You will need to build on what you already have accomplished.

An important element is the setting of requirements and schedules. At this point, we simply do not have the experience with enough teachers, over the necessary length of time, to predict how various groups of teachers will react to different requirements. Since you, as supervisor, know your faculty, you must decide whether it is better to require all performance objectives to be submitted at one time, or have various categories of objectives due on a staggered schedule. For example, should all teachers submit all their objectives on the same date? Should teachers write personal and professional development objectives? If so, should these objectives be due at the same time as the teachers' classroom performance objectives? These are questions about requirements which you are best suited to judge for your teachers, in light of the general climate for objectives in your school.

It is helpful to start the ball rolling before the end of the school year. In this way, the teachers can plan their summer activities to coordinate with next year's objectives. For example, if the teacher is keen on improving his ability to be creative, then he might well decide to attend a summer institute on creativity, such as the one at the University of Buffalo.

At the same time, it is important to keep in mind that next year's objectives are most pertinent and meaningful when the teacher begins in September. He knows his class assignment, who his students are, and who his colleagues are. Thus, it is necessary, in the first few days after the summer recess, to meet with each teacher and confer with him about his performance objectives.

The conference is the time for mutual agreement on the teacher's performance objectives. Not only will you check the adequacy of each objective, but you must look at the totality of the objectives.

During the Conference ask such questions as:

Do they suit the teacher?

Do they suit the situation?

Do they add up to a challenge to the teacher to improve his teaching?

Do they fit in with the school's overall plans for the year?

Do they cover the span of the semester or school year?

Do they include the various types of teacher performance objectives?

If you find that some teachers are having difficulty preparing their performance objectives, you should ask them about seeking help. You can request a colleague to help out or you can help out yourself. It is not wise to let a teacher flounder very long, since the task will become more and more threatening. With help, the teacher can write his objectives, gain direction for his teaching, and get on with the task of accomplishing his objectives.

Once the objectives are mutually agreed upon, it is necessary to indicate this in writing by mutually signing a sheet listing the teacher's performance objectives. The signing is necessary so as to have a written document to refer to later in the year for the guidance and protection of teacher and supervisor.

As supervisor, you should *confer periodically* with the teacher regarding his accomplishments. You can combine the conference with feedback conferences based on your classroom observation. But even if you prefer a separate conference, although this is time consuming, you need to meet with the teacher several times during the year. Periodic conferences will serve as motivation as well as danger signals in case the teacher is way off target. If there is need for remediation, periodic conferences will permit you to take the appropriate steps and even rewrite the teacher's objectives, if necessary.

At the end of the year, you will need to confer with the teacher to make your final achievement assessment. Here, you should draw on your year's observation reports and conference discussions. Just as it is wise to mutually agree on the objectives in September, it is wise to mutually agree to the final assessment in June. In this way, you can set the stage for the writing of next year's performance objectives for continued improvement of the teacher.